SPSS Manual

for

Moore and McCabe's

Introduction to the Practice of Statistics
Third Edition

Paul L. Stephenson
Neal T. Rogness
Justine M. Ritchie
Patricia A. B. Stephenson
Grand Valley State University

W. H. Freeman and Company
New York

SPSS is a registered trademark of SPSS Inc.
Microsoft and Windows are registered trademarks of the Microsoft Corporation.
SPSS screen shots are reprinted with permission from SPSS Inc.
Excel 97 and Word 97 screen shots are reprinted with permission from the Microsoft Corporation.

ISBN 0-7167-3399-4

Printed in the United States of America

First Printing, 1998

Contents

Preface

We have found from personal experience that an ideal way to teach and learn statistics is by engaging students as active learners through exploratory data analysis. Exploratory data analysis is greatly facilitated by using statistical software because it allows students to primarily focus on the interpretation of statistical analyses, not the calculations. SPSS has been regarded as one of the most powerful statistical packages for many years. It performs a wide variety of statistical techniques ranging from descriptive statistics to complex multivariate procedures. In addition, a number of improvements have been made to version 8.0 of SPSS that make it more user friendly. Since most of the features in SPSS 8.0 are mouse driven (requiring no programming), we think students will consider SPSS 8.0 to be an easy-to-use statistical software package.

This manual is a supplement to the third edition of Moore and McCabe's *Introduction to the Practice of Statistics* (IPS). The purpose of this manual is to show students how to perform the statistical procedures discussed in IPS using SPSS 8.0. This manual provides applications and examples for each chapter of the text. The statistical analyses for each example are motivated, demonstrated, and briefly described. You will observe that (for the purpose of consistency with IPS) most of the examples and subsequent discussion come directly from IPS. Step-by-step instructions describing how to carry out statistical analyses using SPSS 8.0 are provided.

We would like to thank Penny Hull, the copy editor for this project, for her editorial suggestions and Patrick Farace, a sponsoring editor for W. H. Freeman and Company, for giving us the opportunity to undertake this project. We would also like to thank Sheila Pomeroy, a statistics student at Grand Valley State University, for reviewing this manual and providing us with feedback from a student's perspective.

Paul Stephenson
Neal Rogness
Justine Ritchie
Patricia Stephenson

Chapter 0. Introduction to SPSS 8.0

This manual is a supplement to *Introduction to the Practice of Statistics*, Third Edition, by David S. Moore and George P. McCabe, which is referred to as IPS throughout the manual. The purpose of this manual is to show students how to perform the statistical procedures discussed in IPS using SPSS 8.0. This manual is not meant to be a comprehensive guide to all procedures available in SPSS.

Throughout this manual, the following conventions are used: (1) variable names are given in boldface italics (e.g., *age*), (2) commands one clicks or text one types are boldface (e.g., click **Statistics**), (3) important statistical terms are boldface, (4) the names of boxes or areas within an SPSS window are in double quotes (e.g., the "Variables Name" box), and (5) in an example number, the digit(s) before the decimal place is the chapter number and the digit(s) after the decimal place is the example number within that chapter (e.g., Example 1.3 is the third example in Chapter 1). Unless otherwise specified, all example, table, and figure numbers refer to examples, tables, and figures within this manual.

This chapter serves as a brief overview of tasks that help one get started in SPSS, such as entering data, reading in data, saving data, printing output, and using SPSS Help.

Section 0.1. Accessing SPSS 8.0

Find out how to access SPSS at your location. Figure 0.1 shows the opening screen in SPSS 8.0 after the software has been activated. Note that in the section labeled "Open an existing file" located within the "SPSS for Windows" window, the most recent files used in SPSS are listed, and they can be easily opened by clicking on the desired file name and then clicking "OK". If, instead, you want to enter data into a new file, you can click on "Type in data" and then click "OK". For new SPSS users, we recommend clicking on "Run the tutorial" to become acquainted with the software package.

The window in the background of Figure 0.1 is the SPSS Data Editor. You will note that the SPSS Data Editor is in a spreadsheet format where columns represent variables and rows represent individual cases or observations. The SPSS Menu bar (**File**, **Edit**, ... , **Help**) appears directly below "Untitled – SPSS Data Editor". Each of these main menu options contains its own submenu of additional options. Throughout this manual, the first step in performing a particular task or analysis often gives the SPSS Menu bar as the starting point (e.g., Click **File**, then click **Open**).

In addition to the Data Editor, the other primary window is the Output window (which is not accessible until after output has been generated). To move between these two windows, select **Window** from the SPSS Main Menu and then click on the name of the desired window. In Figure 0.2, the SPSS Data Editor is the current active window, as shown by the ✔ in front of that window name.

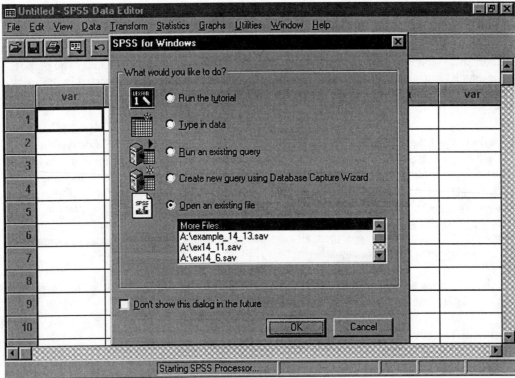

Figure 0.1

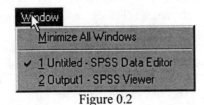

Figure 0.2

Most of the output in SPSS can be generated by clicking on a series of commands using a sequence of pulldown menus. However, it is also possible to generate output by writing a program using SPSS syntax language. The explanation of the syntax language is beyond the scope of this manual. However, the interested reader can learn more about this feature by clicking on **Help** in the SPSS Menu bar, then clicking on **Syntax Guide**. Programs using the SPSS syntax language are presented in Chapters 5 and 6 of this manual.

Section 0.2. Entering Data

Before entering a data set into SPSS, you need to determine whether the variable is quantitative or categorical. A **quantitative** variable assumes numerical values for which arithmetic operations make sense, and a **categorical** variable places an individual into one of several groups or categories. SPSS also uses the variable classifications of nominal, ordinal, or scale. A **nominal** variable is a variable that classifies characteristics about the objects under study into categories. Some examples of nominal variables are eye color, race, and gender. An **ordinal** variable is a variable that classifies characteristics about the objects under study into categories that can be logically ordered. Some examples of ordinal variables are the size of eggs (small, medium, or large) and class standing (freshman, sophomore, junior, or senior). **Scale** variables, collectively referring to both interval and ratio variables, are quantitative variables for which arithmetic operations make sense. Some examples of scale variables are height, weight, and age.

By default, SPSS assumes that any new variable is a scale variable formatted to have a width of 8 digits, 2 of which are decimal places. This is denoted in SPSS by "numeric 8.2".

Suppose you want to enter the data set presented in Example 1.1 into SPSS. The variable in this data set is a categorical and nominal variable. Since this variable does not contain numeric values, you will not be able to enter the data values (Yes, No, or Undecided) into the SPSS Data Editor until the type of the variable has been changed from the default option of numeric 8.2 to another option called "string", which allows text to be entered. For this example, if you want to type "Undecided" as a data value for the variable *vote*, then the width of the variable must be at least 9 characters.

To create this data set in SPSS, follow these steps.

1. Click **File**, click **New**, and then click **Data**. The SPSS Data Editor is cleared.
2. To define the variable to be entered into the data set, double click on the first column header (the [var] button). The "Define Variable" window in Figure 0.3 appears.
3. To change the variable name from the default name of *var00001* to a more appropriate name (such as *vote*), type *vote* into the "Variable Name" box. Variable names in SPSS can be at most 8 characters long containing no embedded blanks.
4. To change the type of the variable, click **Type**. The "Define Variable Type" window in Figure 0.4 appears.
5. Click **String**.
6. To change the width of the variable *vote* from the default width of 8 characters to 9 characters, type **9** in the "Width" box.
7. Click **Continue**.
8. Click **OK**. The variable name *vote* now appears in the SPSS Data Editor.
9. Type in the first value of the variable *vote* and then press the **Enter** key. Continue this process until all the values are entered into the SPSS Data Editor.

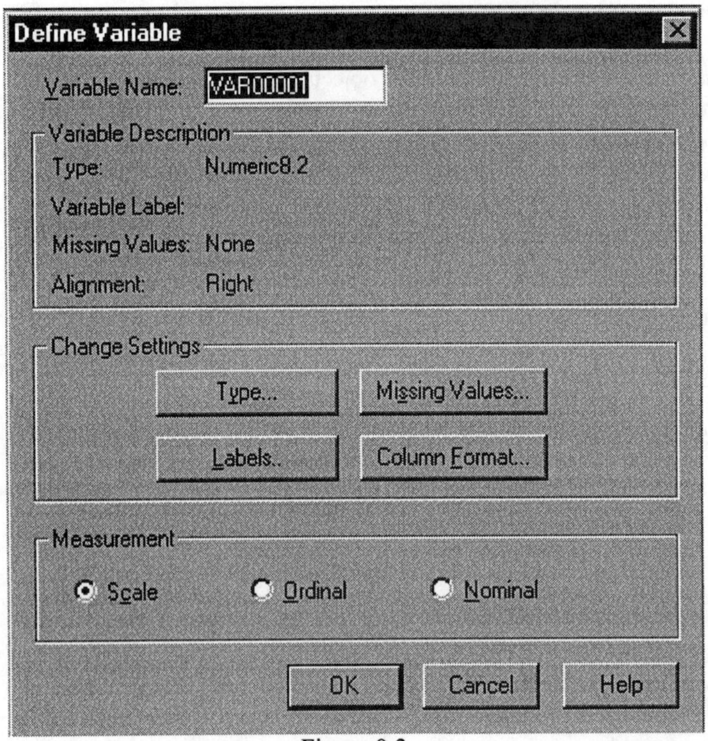

Figure 0.3

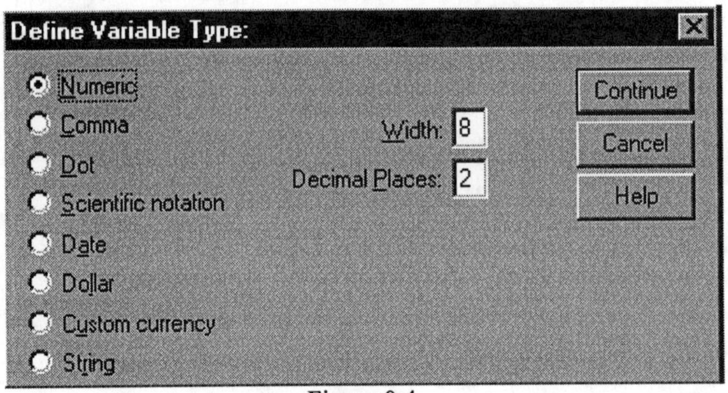

Figure 0.4

Section 0.3. Saving an SPSS Data File

To save an SPSS data file, follow these steps.

1. Click **File** and click **Save as**. The "Save Data As" window appears (see Figure 0.5).
2. If you wish to save the file on disk, click ▼ in the "Save in" box until **3 1/2 Floppy [A:]** appears, and then click on this name. If you prefer to save the file in a different location, continue to click on ▼ until the name of the desired location is found, then click on this location name.
3. By default, SPSS assigns the .sav extension to data files. If you wish to save the data in a format other than an SPSS data file, click ▼ in the "Save as type" box until the name of the desired file type appears, then click on this file type name.
4. In the "File name" box, type in the desired name of the file you are saving. The name **example1_1** is used in Figure 0.5.
5. Make sure a disk is in the A: drive, and then click **Save**.

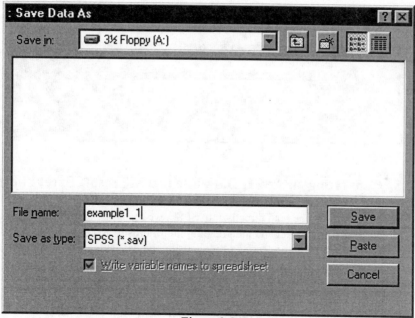

Figure 0.5

Section 0.4. Opening an Existing SPSS Data File from Disk

To open an existing SPSS data file from a disk, follow these steps.

1. Click **File** and click **Open**. The "Open File" window appears (see Figure 0.6).
2. If you wish to open an SPSS data file from a disk in the A: drive, click ▼ in the "Look in" box until **3 1/2 Floppy [A:]** appears, then click on this name. If you prefer to open a file

stored in a different location, continue to click on ▼ until the name of the desired location is
found, then click on this location name.

3. All files with a .sav extension will be listed in the window. Click on the name of the data file
    you wish to open. This name now appears in the "File name" box. In Figure 0.6,
    example1_1.sav is the desired SPSS data file.

4. Click **Open**.

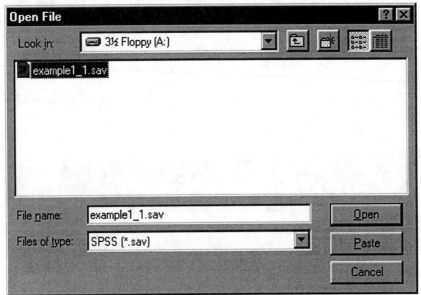

Figure 0.6

Section 0.5. Converting an ASCII Data File to a Microsoft Excel File

Although ASCII data files can be read directly into SPSS, we recommend initially reading the
ASCII data file into Microsoft Excel and then reading the Microsoft Excel file into SPSS. The
following example illustrates the conversion process using the data associated with Table 1.6
(Educational data for 78 seventh-grade students) in IPS, which is contained on the CD-ROM
provided with IPS.

To convert an ASCII text data file into a Microsoft Excel file, follow these steps.

1. Open Microsoft Excel.
2. Click **File** and then click **Open**. The "Open" window appears (see Figure 0.7).
3. Click ▼ in the "Look in" box until you find the name of the drive that contains the ASCII
    text data file and then click on this name. For this example, the drive that contains the ASCII
    text data file of interest is drive D: (see Figure 0.7).
4. Double click on the **Extras** folder, double click on the **Datasets** folder, and then double click
    on the **Chap01** folder.
5. Click ▼ in "Files of type" box, and then click **All Files [*.*]**.

6. Double click **Ta01_006.dat**. The "Text Import Wizard" window opens as shown in Figure 0.8. The "Text Import Wizard" determines that the data are of fixed width (variable values are lined up in columns). As can be seen in the "Start Import at Row" box, the "Text Import Wizard" is set to begin importing data at row 1, which is correct (since no variable names appear as column headings in the data).

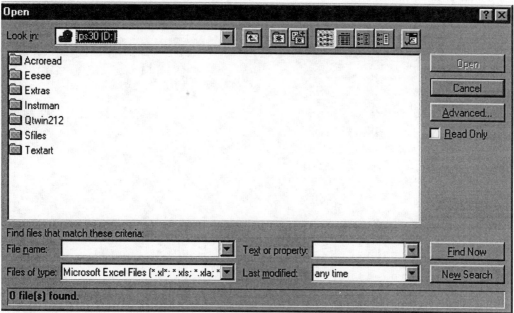

Figure 0.7

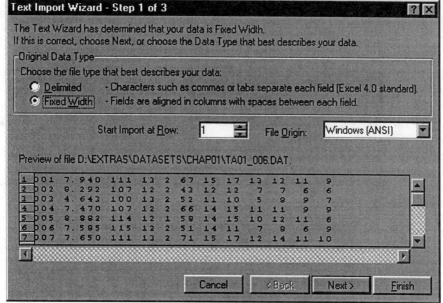

Figure 0.8

7. Click **Next>**. The second window of the "Text Import Wizard" appears, as shown in Figure 0.9. Each column of numbers in the "Data Preview" box represents the different variables in the data set. The "Text Import Wizard" suggests where the column breaks should occur between the variables. Additional column breaks can be inserted by clicking at the desired location within the "Data Preview" box. An existing column break can be removed by double clicking on that column break. The breaks suggested by the "Text Import Wizard" are appropriate for these data.

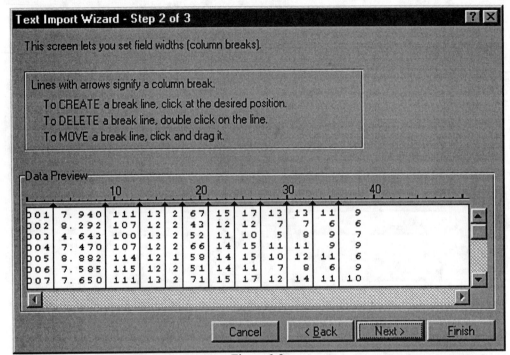

Figure 0.9

8. Click **Next>**. The third window of the "Text Import Window" appears, as shown in Figure 0.10. Here you can exclude variables, if desired, by clicking on the column you do not wish to import and selecting "Do Not Import Column (Skip)" in the "Column Data Format" box. You can also specify the format for each variable. By default, all variables are assigned a General format. We recommend that you retain the General format for variables to provide the most flexibility in SPSS.
9. Click **Finish**. The data will appear in the Microsoft Excel spreadsheet, where the columns represent variables and the rows represent cases. Figure 0.11 shows the first five variables for the first five cases.

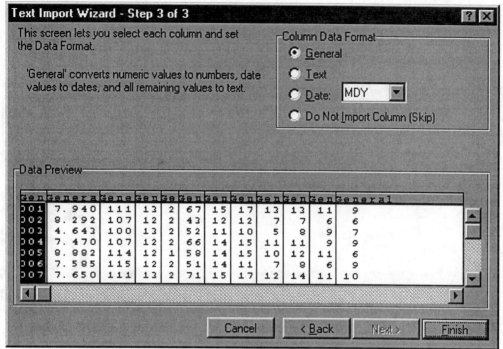

Figure 0.10

	A	B	C	D	E
1	1	7.94	111	13	2
2	2	8.292	107	12	2
3	3	4.643	100	13	2
4	4	7.47	107	12	2
5	5	8.882	114	12	1

Figure 0.11

Section 0.6. Saving a Microsoft Excel Data File in a Format Usable by SPSS

The example used in this section is based on data associated with Table 1.6 (Educational data for 78 seventh-grade students) in IPS, which is contained on the CD-ROM provided with IPS. It is assumed that these data have already been read into Microsoft Excel (see Section 0.5) and Microsoft Excel has been opened.

To save a Microsoft Excel data file in a format usable by SPSS, follow these steps.

1. Click **File** and click **Save as**. The "Save As" window appears (see Figure 0.12).
2. If you wish to save the file on disk, click ▼ in the "Save in" box until **3 ½ Floppy [A:]** appears, then click on this name. If you prefer to save the file in a different location, continue to click on ▼ until the name of the desired location is found, then click on this location name.

9

3. Click ▼ in the "Save as type" box until the file type **Microsoft Excel 4.0 Worksheet [*.xls]** appears, then click on this file type.
4. In the "File Name" box, type in the desired name of the file you are saving. As shown in Figure 0.12, the name **table6_1** is used in this example.

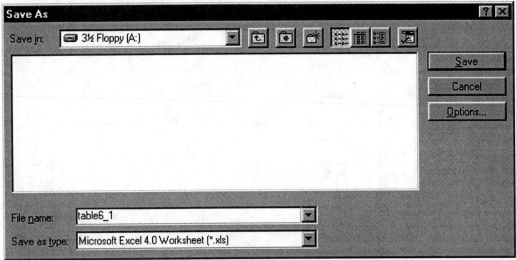

Figure 0.12

5. Make sure a disk is in the A: drive, and then click **Save**.
6. The data file will be saved on the disk in the A: drive. If you are finished with the data file in Microsoft Excel, you can close the file by clicking **File** and then **Close.** If you are finished working in Microsoft Excel, you can exit the program by clicking **File** and then **Exit**.

Section 0.7. Opening a Microsoft Excel Data File in SPSS

The example used in this section is based on data associated with Table 1.6 (Educational data for 78 seventh-grade students) in IPS, which is contained on the CD-ROM provided with IPS. It is assumed that the data have already been read into Microsoft Excel (see Section 0.5) and saved as a Microsoft Excel 4.0 Worksheet (see Section 0.6).

To open a Microsoft Excel data file in SPSS, follow these steps.

1. From the SPSS Data Editor Menu bar, click **File** and then click **Open**. The SPSS "Open File" window appears (see Figure 0.13).
2. Click ▼ in the "Look in" box until the name **3 ½ Floppy [A:]** appears, then click on this name. If the data file was saved in a different location, continue to click on ▼ until the name of the appropriate location appears, and then click on this location name.
3. Click ▼ in the "Files of type" box until the file name type **Excel [*.xls]** appears, and then click on this file type name. The file names of any Microsoft Excel files stored on the A: drive will appear in the large center box.

10

4. Click on the name of the file you wish to open in SPSS. The desired file name will appear in the "File name" box. In the example, as shown in Figure 0.13, the name of the desired Microsoft Excel file is **table6_1.xls**.

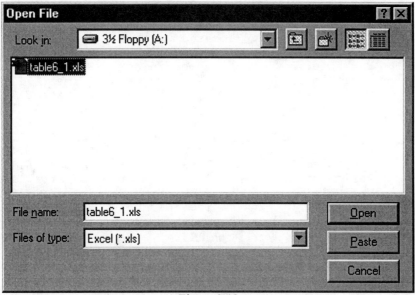

Figure 0.13

5. Click **Open**. The "Opening File Options" window appears, as shown in Figure 0.14. If the data set contains the variable names in the first row, click on the "Read variable names" box so that a check mark appears in the box. For this example, the variable names do not appear in the first row of the data set (see Figure 0.11); therefore, this box should remain unchecked.

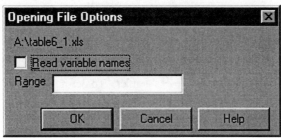

Figure 0.14

6. Click **OK**.
7. After the data are read into SPSS, the Output window of SPSS becomes the active window, and it gives a log containing the name of each variable read into SPSS, as well as the type and format of each variable (see Figure 0.15). Note that each variable in the data set is formatted as numeric 11.2, which means that the width of each variable is 11 digits including 2 digits for decimal places.
8. To go to the actual data contained in the Data Editor, click **Window**, then click **1 Untitled – SPSS Data Editor**. Figure 0.16 shows the first five variables for the first five cases. Other

than the number of digits for decimal places for each of the variables, the values agree with those shown in Figure 0.11.

```
Data written to the working file
12 variables and 78 cases written.
Variable: A          Type: Number      Format: F11.2
Variable: B          Type: Number      Format: F11.2
Variable: C          Type: Number      Format: F11.2
Variable: D          Type: Number      Format: F11.2
Variable: E          Type: Number      Format: F11.2
Variable: F          Type: Number      Format: F11.2
Variable: G          Type: Number      Format: F11.2
Variable: H          Type: Number      Format: F11.2
Variable: I          Type: Number      Format: F11.2
Variable: J          Type: Number      Format: F11.2
Variable: K          Type: Number      Format: F11.2
Variable: L          Type: Number      Format: F11.2
```

Figure 0.15

	a	b	c	d	e
1	1.00	7.94	111.00	13.00	2.00
2	2.00	8.29	107.00	12.00	2.00
3	3.00	4.64	100.00	13.00	2.00
4	4.00	7.47	107.00	12.00	2.00
5	5.00	8.88	114.00	12.00	1.00

Figure 0.16

Note: Variable a is the observation number, variable b is GPA, variable c is IQ, variable d does not appear in Table 1.6 in IPS, and variable e is gender. To define these variables, see Section 0.8.

Section 0.8. Defining a Variable

You might be interested in changing the default SPSS variable names to more appropriate variable names. **Variable names** in SPSS can be at most 8 characters long containing no embedded blanks. Because of the limitation in the number of characters allowed for a variable name, you might be interested in providing a **variable label**, a descriptive explanation of the variable name. Variable labels can be at most 256 characters long and can contain embedded blanks. The use of the variable label can make the SPSS output more user friendly in appearance.

When the data from Table 1.6 from IPS were read in from the CD-ROM (via Microsoft Excel, as explained in Section 0.5), the default variable names were a, b, c, d, e, etc. Variable a is the

12

observation number, variable **b** is GPA, variable **c** is IQ, variable **d** does not appear in Table 1.6 in IPS, variable **e** is gender, etc. In the SPSS Data Editor, the values for **gender** are 1.00 or 2.00, where 1.00 = Female and 2.00 = Male. To make the SPSS output more user friendly in appearance, you can add **value labels** to the variable **gender**. Without value labels, the SPSS output will represent the variable **gender** as "1.00" and "2.00", but with value labels, **gender** will instead appear as "Female" and "Male", respectively.

To define a variable in SPSS (such as declaring the variable name, declaring the variable type, adding variable labels and value labels, and declaring the measurement type), follow these steps. The steps use variable **e** as an example.

1. Click on the column heading for the variable **e** in the "SPSS Data Editor" window, click **Data**, and then click **Define Variable**. The "Define Variable" window in Figure 0.17 appears. Note: You can also get to the "Define Variable" window by double clicking on the column heading for the variable **e** in the "SPSS Data Editor" window.

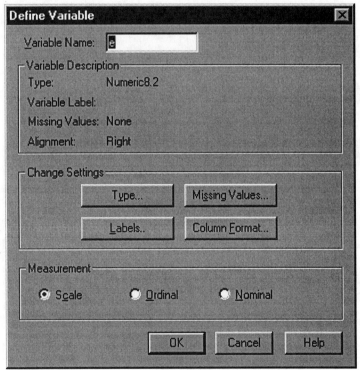

Figure 0.17

2. Type an appropriate variable name, such as **gender**, in the "Variable Name" box.
3. Select the appropriate measurement from the options available in the "Measurement" box: scale, ordinal, or nominal (see Section 0.2 for definitions). The default option is scale. For the variable **gender**, click **Nominal**.
4. If you are interested in changing the width of the variable or the number of decimal places, click **Type**. For instance, with the variable **gender**, decimal places are not necessary. The "Define Variable Type" window in Figure 0.18 appears. Change the value in the "Decimal

Places" box from 2 to **0**. If one is interested in changing the width of the variable, then change the value in the "Width" box. Click **Continue**.

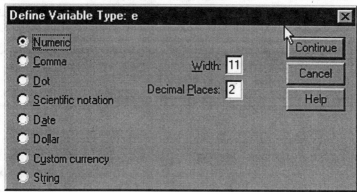

Figure 0.18

5. If you are interested in adding a variable label and value labels to the variable, click **Label**. The SPSS window in Figure 0.19 appears. In the "Variable Label" box, type in an appropriate variable label, such as **Gender of Respondents**. Press the **Tab** key. In the "Value" box, type **1** and then press the **Tab** key. In the "Value Label" box, type **Female**, and then click **Add**. The cursor will return to the "Value" box. Type **2**, then press the **Tab** key, then type **Male**. Click **Add**.

6. Click **Continue**.

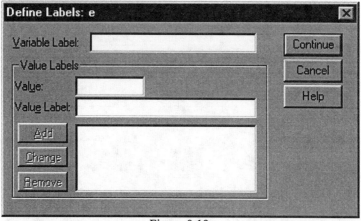

Figure 0.19

7. Click **OK**. The variable name *e* has been replaced with *gender* in the SPSS Data Editor. Note that the data appear unchanged in the SPSS Data Editor (the values of "1" and "2" still appear under the variable *gender*). However, this change will be apparent in the SPSS output window.

Section 0.9. Recoding a Variable

Some of the analyses to be performed in SPSS will require that a categorical variable be entered into SPSS as a numeric variable. If the variable has already been entered as string into the SPSS Data Editor, you can easily create a new variable that contains the same information as the string variable but is numeric simply by recoding the variable. For example, for the data set entered in Section 0.2 (from Example 1.1), you might want to recode the variable *vote* into a numeric variable, called *votenum*, by assigning Yes = 1, No = 2, and Undecided = 3.

To recode a variable into a different variable (the recommended option), follow these steps.

1. Click **Transform**, click **Recode**, and then click **Into Different Variables**. The "Recode into Different Variables" window in Figure 0.20 appears.

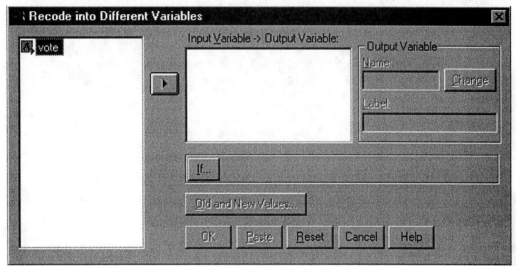

Figure 0.20

2. Click *vote*, and then click ▸ to move *vote* into the "Input Variable -> Output Variable" box.
3. In the "Name" box within the "Output Variable" box, type in a new variable name such as *votenum*.
4. Click **Change**.
5. Click **Old and New Values**. The "Recode into Different Variables: Old and New Values" window in Figure 0.21 appears.
6. In the "Value" box within the "Old Value" box, type **Yes** (the value has to be entered into this box <u>exactly</u> as it appears in the SPSS Data Editor). In the "Value" box in the "New Value" box, type **1**. Click **Add**. **'Yes'→1** appears in the "Old→ New" box. In the "Value" box within the "Old Value" box, type **No** (the value has to be entered into this box <u>exactly</u> as it appears in the SPSS Data Editor). In the "Value" box in the "New Value" box, type **2**. Click **Add**. **'No'→2** appears in the "Old→ New" box. In the "Value" box within the "Old Value" box, type **Undecided** (the value has to be entered into this box <u>exactly</u> as it appears in the SPSS Data Editor). In the "Value" box in the "New Value" box, type **3**. Click **Add**. **'Undecided'→3** appears in the "Old→ New" box. Click **Continue**.

15

7. Click **OK**. The new variable *votenum* appears in the SPSS Data Editor. To add value labels to the variable *votenum*, see section 0.8.

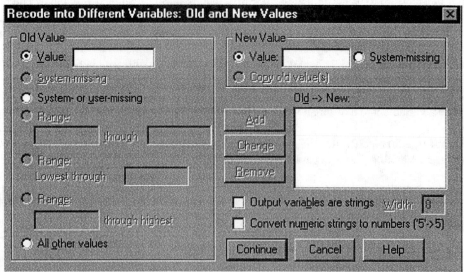

Figure 0.21

Section 0.10. Printing in SPSS

The remaining chapters in this manual introduce various statistical techniques including the generation of summary statistics (called "Output") and the creation of graphs (called "Charts"). Once the desired results have been obtained, it is often of interest to print the results.

Printing Data in SPSS

To print out the data in the SPSS Data Editor, follow these steps.

1. Make the SPSS Data Editor the active window.
2. Click **File**, then click **Print**. The "Print Untitled" window shown in Figure 0.22 appears.

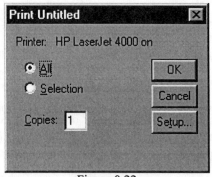

Figure 0.22

3. SPSS assumes that you want to print the entire data set. If you wish to print only a subset of the data (e.g., only one variable), you must first click on the appropriate column heading(s). If this is done, "Selection" in Figure 0.22 will be highlighted rather than "All".
4. Click **OK**.

Printing Output and Charts in SPSS

To print out SPSS output and/or SPSS charts, follow these steps.

1. Make the "SPSS Output" window the active window.
2. If you want to print all of the output, including graphs, click the Output icon (Output), which appears at the top of the left-hand window. All output is highlighted, as shown in Figure 0.23.

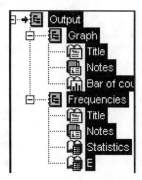

Figure 0.23

3. If you want to print only a specific portion of the output, such as the bar chart only, click on that icon only (see Figure 0.24).

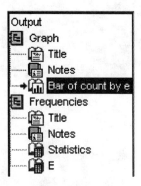

Figure 0.24

4. Click **File**, click **Print**, and then click **OK**.
5. After the output has been printed, it can be deleted. This is accomplished by first highlighting the portion of the output you wish to delete. For example, you can highlight all the output, as

shown in Figure 0.23, or highlight a specific icon, as shown in Figure 0.24. Then after the desired output has been selected, the output can be deleted by pressing the **Delete** key.

Section 0.11. Copying from SPSS into Microsoft Word 97

To copy a chart from SPSS into Microsoft Word 97, follow these steps. (Note: It is assumed that Microsoft Word 97 has already been opened.)

1. In the "Output SPSS Viewer" window, select the chart to be copied by clicking on the icon that appears in the left-hand side of the window. For example, the **Bar of count by e** icon shown in Figure 0.24.
2. Click **Edit** and then click **Copy**.
3. In Microsoft Word 97, position the cursor at the desired place in the document, click **Edit** and then click **Paste**.
4. If you are interested in resizing the picture, click on the picture and place the cursor on one of the little squares appearing at the corners of the picture. Using the right mouse button, drag the cursor in or out depending on how you want to resize the picture.
5. To begin typing in Microsoft Word 97, click on any area outside the chart within the document.

To copy a table from SPSS into Microsoft Word 97, follow these steps.

1. In the "Output SPSS Viewer" window, select the table to be copied by clicking on the icon that appears in the left-hand side of the window. For example, the **E** icon (a frequency table for the variable *e*) shown in Figure 0.24.
2. Click **Edit** and then click **Copy**.
3. In Microsoft Word 97, position the cursor at the desired place in the document, click **Edit** and then click **Paste Special**. The "Paste Special" window in Figure 0.25 appears.

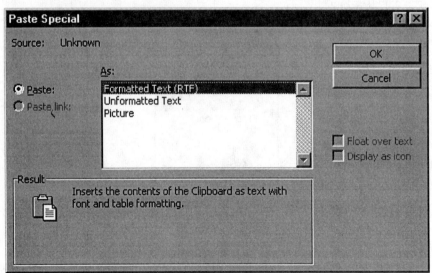

Figure 0.25

4. Click **Picture** and then click **Float over text**. The ✔ in front of "Float over text" disappears.
5. Click **OK**.
6. To begin typing in Microsoft Word 97, click on any area outside the table within the document.

Section 0.12. Using SPSS Help

SPSS has extensive and useful on-line help. Suppose you want to know the steps needed to obtain a boxplot using SPSS and no manual is available. This information can be obtained using the help function of SPSS by following these steps.

1. Click **Help**, and then click **Topics**. The "Help Topics" window appears as shown in Figure 0.26.

Figure 0.26

2. Click **Index** and type **Box** in the "Type the first few letters of the word you're looking for" box. Figure 0.27 shows the list of potential terms from which to choose.
3. Double click **obtaining** under "boxplots". The directions entitled "To Obtain Simple and Clustered Boxplots" appear in the "How To" window (see Figure 0.28).
4. To print the directions, click **Print**.
5. To exit SPSS Help, click ⊠ in the upper right corner of the "How To" window.

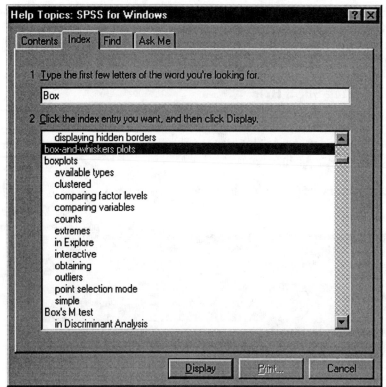

Figure 0.27

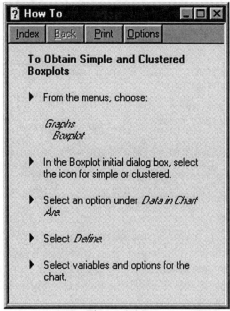

Figure 0.28

Chapter 1. Looking at Data — Distributions

Section 1.1. Displaying Distributions with Graphs

Statistical tools and ideas help us examine data. This examination is called exploratory data analysis. This section introduces the notion of using graphical displays to perform exploratory data analysis. The graphical display used to summarize a single variable will depend upon the type of variable being studied (i.e., whether the variable is categorical or quantitative). For categorical variables, **frequency tables**, **bar charts**, and **pie charts** will be examined. For quantitative variables, **stemplots**, **histograms**, and **time plots** will be examined.

Frequency Tables, Bar Charts, and Pie Charts for Ungrouped Categorical Data

The notion of obtaining a frequency table, a bar chart, and a pie chart for a small data set containing a single categorical variable is introduced here. The frequency table reports the frequencies and percentages for each of the categories of the categorical variable. The bar chart and pie chart are appropriate graphical displays used to describe a single categorical variable.

Example 1.1

Twenty randomly selected faculty members were asked if they would vote in favor of the new General Education requirements proposed to be implemented within the next two years. The data are given in Table 1.1.

Table 1.1 Votes on General Education Requirements Proposal

Yes	Yes	No	Undecided	No
Yes	No	Yes	Undecided	Yes
Yes	No	Yes	Undecided	No
No	No	Yes	Undecided	Undecided

Summarize the data set using appropriate descriptive statistics and appropriate graphs.

The SPSS Data Editor contains a single variable called *vote*, which is declared type string of length 9 (see Section 0.8).

Frequency Tables

To create a frequency table for a categorical variable, follow these steps.

1. Click **Statistics**, click **Summarize**, and then click **Frequencies**. The SPSS window in Figure 1.1 appears.
2. Click *vote*, then click ▶ to move *vote* into the "Variable(s)" box.
3. Click **OK**.

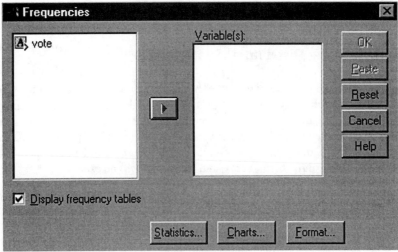

Figure 1.1

Table 1.2 is part of the resulting SPSS output.

VOTE

		Frequency	Percent	Valid Percent	Cumulative Percent
Valid	No	7	35.0	35.0	35.0
	Undecided	5	25.0	25.0	60.0
	Yes	8	40.0	40.0	100.0
	Total	20	100.0	100.0	

Table 1.2

Example 1.1 (cont.)   Seven faculty members, or 35% of those sampled, would not vote in favor of the new General Education requirements. Five faculty members, or 25% of those sampled, are undecided about how they would vote. Eight faculty members, or 40% of those sampled, would vote in favor of the new General Education requirements. The Cumulative Percent is the percent of the current category plus the percents of all the categories above it.

Bar Charts

To create a bar chart for a categorical variable, follow these steps.

1. Click **Graphs** and then click **Bar**. The SPSS window in Figure 1.2 appears.
2. Click **Define**. The SPSS window in Figure 1.3 appears.
3. Click *vote*, then click ▶ to move *vote* into the "Category Axis" box.

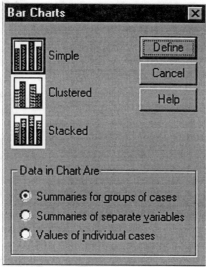

Figure 1.2

4. By default, the bars represent the number of cases. If you are interested in the *y* axis being labeled as "Percent" rather than "Count", click **% of cases** in the "Bars Represent" box.

5. If you are interested in including a title or a footnote on the chart, click **Titles**. The SPSS window in Figure 1.4 appears. In the properly labeled box ("Title" or "Footnote"), type in the desired information. Click **Continue**.

6. Click **OK**.

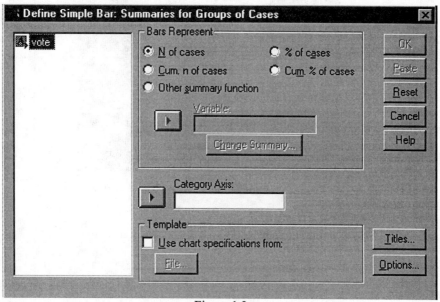

Figure 1.3

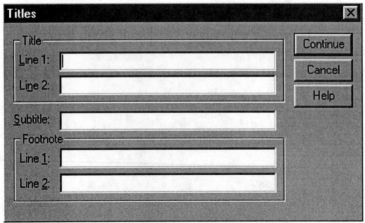

Figure 1.4

Figure 1.5 is the resulting SPSS output.

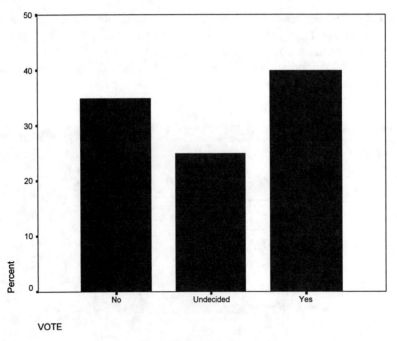

Figure 1.5

Editing Bar Charts

To have the numbers appear within the bars, follow these steps.

1. Double click on the bar chart in the "Output 1 – SPSS Viewer" window. The bar chart now appears in the "Chart 1 – SPSS Chart Editor" window, which has new menu and tool bars.

24

2. Click ▣. The SPSS window in Figure 1.6 appears.

Figure 1.6

3. Click on the box in front of the **Framed** option. "None" is the default option.
4. Click **Apply All**.
5. Click **Close**.
6. If you are finished editing the chart, click **File** and then click **Close** to return to the "Output 1 – SPSS Viewer" window.

To change the color of an area within the chart, follow these steps.

1. The chart needs to be in the "Chart 1 – SPSS Chart Editor" window.
2. Click on the area within the chart for which a change in color is desired, for instance, the bars in the bar chart.
3. Click ▣. The SPSS window in Figure 1.7 appears.

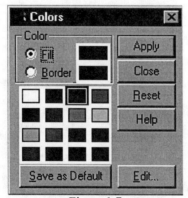

Figure 1.7

4. Make sure that "Fill" rather than "Border" is selected within the "Color" box. Click on the desired color for the fill, for instance, light gray.
5. Click **Apply**.
6. Click **Close**.
7. If you are finished editing the chart, click **File** and then click **Close** to return to the "Output 1 – SPSS Viewer" window.

To change the pattern of an area within the chart, follow these steps.

1. The chart needs to be in the "Chart 1 – SPSS Chart Editor" window.
2. Click on the area within the chart for which a change in pattern is desired, for instance, the bars in the bar chart.
3. Click . The SPSS window in Figure 1.8 appears.

Figure 1.8

4. Click the desired pattern.
5. Click **Apply**.
6. Click **Close**.
7. If you are finished editing the chart, click **File** and then click **Close** to return to the "Output 1 – SPSS Viewer" window.

Figure 1.9 is the resulting SPSS output after adding the numbers inside the bars and changing the color of the bars to light gray.

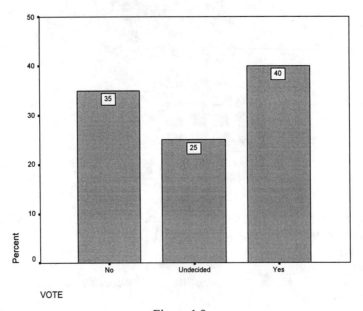

Figure 1.9

Pie Charts

To create a pie chart for a categorical variable, follow these steps.

1. Click **Graphs** and then click **Pie**. The SPSS window in Figure 1.10 appears.

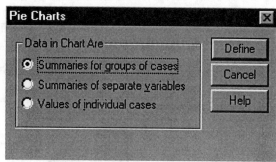

Figure 1.10

2. Click **Define**. The SPSS window in Figure 1.11 appears.

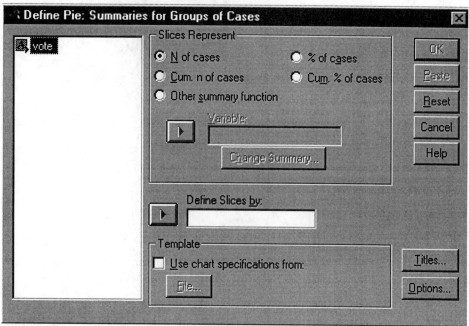

Figure 1.11

3. Click *vote*, then click ▸ to move *vote* into the "Define Slices by" box.
4. By default, the slices represent the number of cases. If you are interested in the slices representing the percents rather than the counts, click **% of cases** in the "Slices Represent" box. However, the same pie chart will appear.

5. If you are interested in including a title or a footnote on the chart, click **Titles**. The "Titles" window shown in Figure 1.4 appears. In the properly labeled box ("Title" or "Footnote"), type in the desired information. Click **Continue**.
6. Click **OK**.

Figure 1.12 is the resulting SPSS output (except for the difference in the color scheme), after having selected **N of cases** rather than **% of cases** in the "Slices Represent" box. To change the color of a pie slice, follow the directions about changing the color in the Editing Bar Charts section.

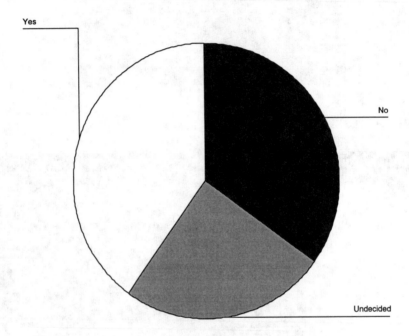

Figure 1.12

Editing Pie Charts

By default, only the category labels of the categorical variable appear on the pie chart. To add the counts and percentages to the pie slices, follow these steps.

1. Double click on the pie chart in the "Output 1 – SPSS Viewer" window. The pie chart now appears in the "Chart 1 – SPSS Chart Editor" window, which has new menu and tool bars.
2. Click **Chart** (from the new menu bar) and then click **Options**. The SPSS window in Figure 1.13 appears.
3. In the "Labels" box, click **Values** and then click **Percents**. The counts and percents appear on the outside of the pie chart beside the category text. If this is the desired format for the output, then skip to step 7.

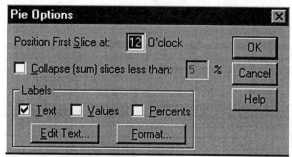
Figure 1.13

4. If you would like the numbers to appear inside the slices, then click **Format**. The SPSS
    window in Figure 1.14 appears.

Figure 1.14

5. Click ▼ located next to the "Position" box until **Numbers inside, text outside** is highlighted.
6. Click **Continue**.
7. Click **OK**.
8. If you are finished editing the chart, click **File** and then click **Close** to return to the "Output 1
    – SPSS Viewer" window.

Figure 1.15 is the resulting SPSS output after adding the counts and percents inside the pie slices
and changing the colors of the slices. To change the color or the pattern fill of a pie slice, follow
the directions about changing the color or the fill in the Editing Bar Charts section.

Bar Charts and Pie Charts for Grouped Categorical Data

This section introduces the notion of obtaining bar charts and pie charts for large data sets
containing a single categorical variable, where the information for the single categorical variable

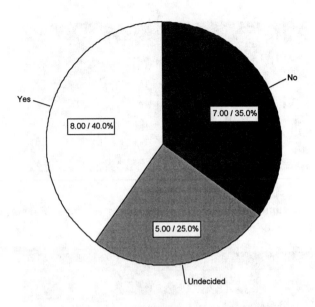

Figure 1.15

has been entered into the SPSS Data Editor as grouped data.

**Example 1.2
(IPS pp. 6–7)**

According to the 1996 *Statistical Abstract of the United States*, the marital distribution for all Americans age 18 and over during 1995 was the following: 43.9 million never married, 116.7 million married, 13.4 million widowed, and 17.6 million divorced.

Summarize the data set using appropriate graphs.

Table 1.3 shows how the data were entered into SPSS.

	marstat	count
1	nevermar	43.9
2	married	116.7
3	widowed	13.4
4	divorced	17.6

Table 1.3

The scale of measurement for *marstat* was nominal (type string 8) and for *count* was scale (type numeric 8.1). The variable *marstat* was labeled as

30

Example 1.2
(cont.)
"Marital Status" and appropriate value labels were given to each value (e.g., "nevermar" was given the value label of "Never married"). For labeling variables, follow the directions given in Section 0.8.

Bar Charts

To create a bar chart for a categorical variable that has been entered as grouped data, follow these steps.

1. Click **Graphs** and then click **Bar**. The SPSS window shown in Figure 1.2 appears.
2. Click **Values of individual cases** and then click **Define**. The SPSS window in Figure 1.16 appears.

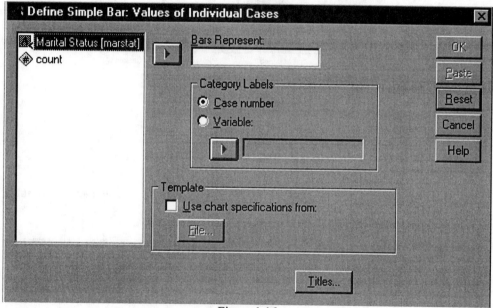

Figure 1.16

3. Click **Variable** in the "Category Labels" box. Click *marstat* and then click ▸ to move *marstat* into the "Variable" box.
4. Click *count* and then click ▸ to move *count* into the "Bars Represent" box.
5. If you want to include a title or a footnote on the chart, click **Titles**. The "Titles" window shown in Figure 1.4 appears. In the properly labeled box ("Title" or "Footnote"), type in the desired information. For this example, the following footnote was used: **Bar Graph of the Marital Status of U.S. Adults**. Click **Continue**.
6. Click **OK**.

Figure 1.17 is the resulting SPSS output. To add numbers to the bars or to change the color or the pattern fill of the bars, follow the directions given in Example 1.1 about editing bar charts.

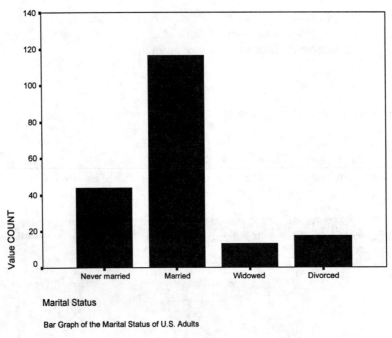

Marital Status

Bar Graph of the Marital Status of U.S. Adults

Figure 1.17

Pie Charts

To create a pie chart for a categorical variable that has been entered as grouped data, follow these steps.

1. Click **Graphs** and then click **Pie**. The "Pie Charts" window shown in Figure 1.10 appears.
2. Click **Values of individual cases** in the "Data in Chart Are" box and then click **Define**. The SPSS window in Figure 1.18 appears.
3. Click **Variable** in the "Slice Labels" box. Click *marstat* and then click ▸ to move *marstat* into the "Variable" box.
4. Click *count* and then click ▸ to move *count* into the "Slices Represent" box.
5. If you want to include a title or a footnote on the chart, click **Titles**. The "Titles" window shown in Figure 1.4 appears. In the properly labeled box ("Title" or "Footnote"), type in the desired information. For this example, the following footnote was used: **Pie Chart of the Same Data**. Click **Continue**.
6. Click **OK**.

Figure 1.19 is the resulting SPSS output (except for the difference in the color scheme). To add numbers to the pie slices or change the color or the pattern fill of the pie slices, follow the directions given in Example 1.1 about editing pie charts.

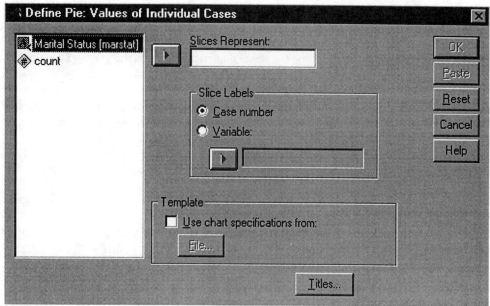

Figure 1.18

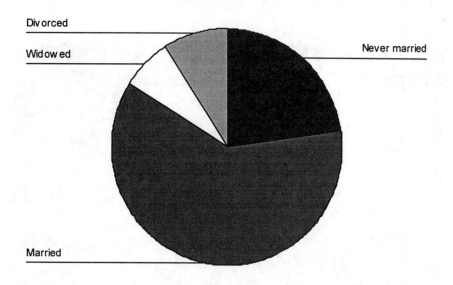

Pie Chart of the Same Data

Figure 1.19

33

Stemplots

A stemplot (also called a stem-and-leaf plot) gives a quick picture of the shape of the distribution for a quantitative variable while including the actual numerical values in the graph. Stemplots work best for small numbers of observations that are all greater than zero.

**Example 1.3
(IPS Ex. 1.5)**

A marketing consultant observed 50 consecutive shoppers at a supermarket. One variable of interest was how much each shopper spent in the store. Table 1.4 contains the data (in dollars), arranged in increasing order.

The SPSS Data Editor contains a single variable called *spending*, which is declared type numeric 8.2.

Table 1.4 Supermarket Shopping Data

3.11	8.88	9.26	10.81	12.69	13.78	15.23	15.62	17.00
17.39	18.36	18.43	19.27	19.50	19.54	20.16	20.59	22.22
23.04	24.47	24.58	25.13	26.24	26.26	27.65	28.06	28.08
28.38	32.03	34.98	36.37	38.64	39.16	41.02	42.97	44.08
44.67	45.40	46.69	48.65	50.39	52.75	54.80	59.07	61.22
70.32	82.70	85.76	86.37	93.34				

To create a stemplot of this distribution, follow these steps.

1. Click **Statistics**, click **Summarize**, and then click **Explore**. The SPSS window in Figure 1.20 appears.

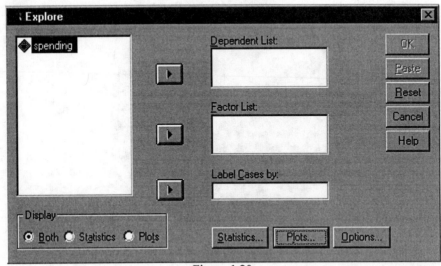

Figure 1.20

2. Click *spending*, then click ▶ to move *spending* into the "Dependent List" box.
3. By default, the "Display" box in the lower left corner has "Both" selected. Click **Plots**.
4. Click **Plots** located next to the "Options" button. The SPSS window in Figure 1.21 appears.

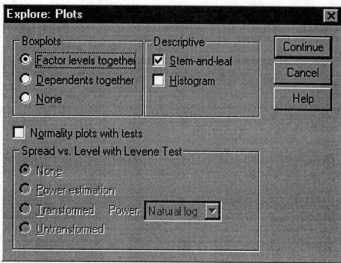

Figure 1.21

5. Click **None** within the "Boxplots" box. Be sure that a ✔ appears in front of "Stem-and-leaf" within the "Descriptive" box.
6. Click **Continue**.
7. Click **OK**.

Part of the resulting SPSS output is shown in Table 1.5.

```
           SPENDING Stem-and-Leaf Plot

    Frequency      Stem &  Leaf
        3.00          0 .  389
       12.00          1 .  023557788999
       13.00          2 .  0023445667888
        5.00          3 .  24689
        7.00          4 .  1244568
        4.00          5 .  0249
        1.00          6 .  1
        1.00          7 .  0
        1.00          8 .  2
        3.00 Extremes      (>=86)

    Stem width:      10.00
    Each leaf:        1 case(s)
```

Table 1.5

Example 1.3 (cont.)

The stemplot was put together by truncating the decimal places. The amount of money spent ranged from $3 to $93. The tens of dollars were used as the stems and the dollars as the leaves. The distribution of supermarket spending is skewed to the right and unimodal. According to the stemplot, there are three extreme observations above $86.

Histograms

A histogram breaks the range of values of a quantitative variable into intervals and displays only the count or the percent of the observations that fall into each interval. You can choose any convenient number of intervals, but you should always choose intervals of equal width.

Example 1.4
(IPS pp. 17–18)

The first reasonably accurate measurements of the speed of light were made over 100 years ago by A. A. Michelson and Simon Newcomb. Newcomb measured the time in seconds that a light signal took to pass from his laboratory on the Potomac River to a mirror at the base of the Washington Monument and back, a total distance of about 7400 meters. Table 1.6 contains 66 measurements made by Newcomb between July and September 1882.

Table 1.6 Newcomb's Measurements of the Passage Time of Light

28	22	36	26	28	28
26	24	32	30	27	24
33	21	36	32	31	25
24	25	28	36	27	32
34	30	25	26	26	25
− 44	23	21	30	33	29
27	29	28	22	26	27
16	31	29	36	32	28
40	19	37	23	32	29
− 2	24	25	27	24	16
29	20	28	27	39	23

Newcomb's first measurement of the passage time of light was 0.000024828 second, or 24,828 nanoseconds. There are 10^9 nanoseconds in a second. The entries in Table 1.6 record only the deviation from 24,800 nanoseconds. The entry − 44 stands for 24,756 nanoseconds.

The SPSS Data Editor contains a single variable called *light*, which is declared type numeric 8.2.

To create a frequency histogram of this distribution, follow these steps.

1. Click **Graphs** and then click **Histogram**. The SPSS window in Figure 1.22 appears.
2. Click *light*, then click ▶ to move *light* to the "Variable" box.
3. If you want to include a title or a footnote on the chart, click **Titles**. The "Titles" window shown in Figure 1.4 appears. In the properly labeled box ("Title" or "Footnote"), type in the desired information. Click **Continue**.
4. Click **OK**.

Figure 1.23 is the default histogram created by SPSS.

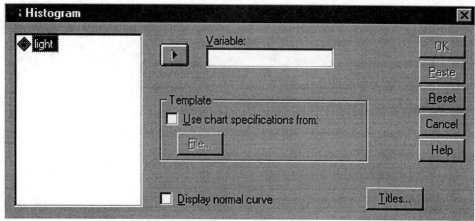

Figure 1.22

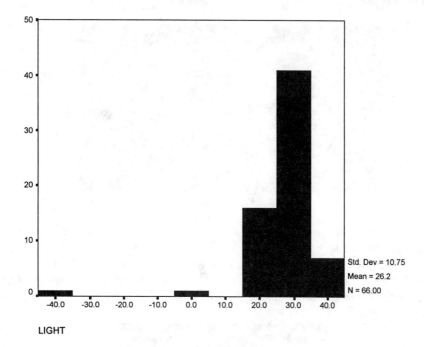

LIGHT

Figure 1.23

Editing Histograms

To obtain a picture of the distribution similar to that shown in IPS Figure 1.5 on page 17, the histogram can be edited. To edit the histogram, double click on the histogram in the "Output 1 – SPSS Viewer" window. The histogram now appears in the "Chart 1 – SPSS Chart Editor" window, which has new menu and tool bars.

To make changes to the x axis (such as changing the title and changing the class width of the bars), follow these steps.

1. Click **Chart** and then click **Axis**. The SPSS window in Figure 1.24 appears.

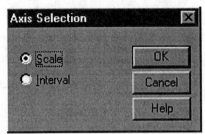

Figure 1.24

2. Click **Interval** and then click **OK**. The SPSS window in Figure 1.25 appears.

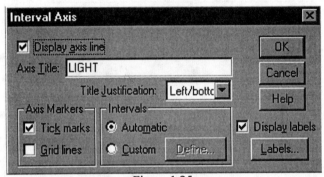

Figure 1.25

3. To change the title of the axis, replace LIGHT with the desired axis title, for instance, **Passage Time of Light**.
4. To center the axis title, click ▼ in the "Title Justification" box and click **Center**.
5. To change the range of values on the x axis and/or the class width of the bars, click **Custom** and then click **Define** located within the "Intervals" box. The SPSS window in Figure 1.26 appears.

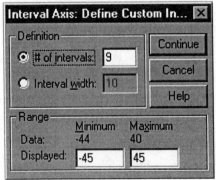

Figure 1.26

6. To change the class width, for instance to 5, click **Interval width** and then type **5** in the "Interval width" box.
7. To change the range of the *x* axis, for instance to – 60 to 60, replace – 45 with – **60** in the "Minimum Displayed" box and replace 45 with **60** in the "Maximum Displayed" box.
8. Click **Continue**.
9. Because the class width of each bar has been decreased, there are more numbers appearing on the *x* axis, making the labels extremely difficult to read. To edit the number of labels appearing on the *x* axis, click **Labels** in the "Interval Axis" window (see Figure 1.25). The SPSS window in Figure 1.27 appears.

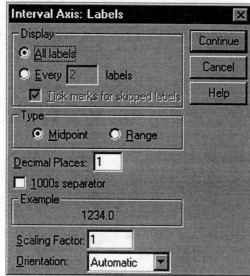
Figure 1.27

10. Click **Every ☐ labels** in the "Display" box. Replace 2 with **4** in the "Every labels" box.
11. Click **Tick marks for skipped labels**. The ✔ disappears.
12. Click ▼ in the "Orientation" box and then click **Horizontal**.
13. Click **Continue**.
14. Click **OK**.

To make changes to the *y* axis (such as adding an axis title and changing the spacing of the tick marks), follow these steps.

1. Click **Chart** and then click **Axis**. The "Axis Select" window shown in Figure 1.24 appears.
2. Click **Scale** and then click **OK**. The SPSS window in Figure 1.28 appears.
3. To label the *y* axis, type the desired label in the "Axis Title" box, such as **Frequency**.
4. To center the axis title, click ▼ in the "Title Justification" box and click **Center**.
5. To change the spacing of the tick marks on the *y* axis from 10 to 5, replace 10 with **5** in the "Major Divisions Increment" box.
6. Click **OK**.

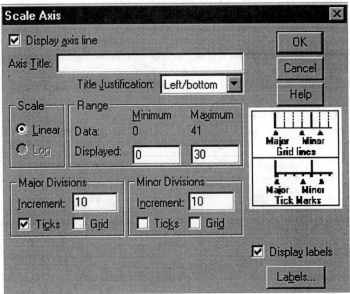

Figure 1.28

To remove the descriptive statistics (Std. Dev., Mean, and N) in the legend, follow these steps.

1.   Click **Chart** and then click **Legend**. The SPSS window in Figure 1.29 appears.

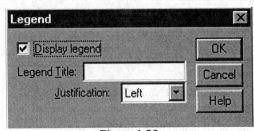

Figure 1.29

2.   Click **Display legend**. The ✓ disappears.
3.   Click **OK**.

Figure 1.30 is the resulting SPSS output after making changes to the *x* and *y* axes. To add numbers to the bars or change the color or the fill of the bars, follow the directions given in Example 1.1 about editing bar charts.

Example 1.4 (cont.)	The histogram shows that Newcomb's data do have a symmetric unimodal distribution — but there are two low outliers (the two negative values of − 2 and − 44) that stand outside this pattern, possibly suggesting a left-skewed distribution.

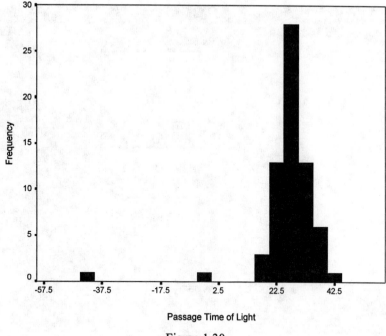

Figure 1.30

Time Plots

Many interesting data sets are time series, measurements of a variable taken at regular intervals over time. When data are collected over time, it is a good idea to plot the observations in time order. A time plot puts time on the horizontal scale of the plot and the quantitative variable of interest on the vertical scale.

Example 1.5
(IPS pp. 18–19)

We can gain more insight into Newcomb's data (see Example 1.4) by examining a time plot. Column 1 in Table 1.6 gives the first 11 measurements made by Newcomb, the second column gives the next 11 measurements made by Newcomb, etc. The time plot for this data set will plot Newcomb's passage times of light against the sequence number, where the sequence number reveals the order in which the observations were recorded.

The SPSS Data Editor contains a single variable called *light*, which is declared type numeric 8.2.

To obtain a time plot of a quantitative variable against its sequence number, follow these steps.

1. Click **Graphs** and then click **Sequence**. The SPSS window in Figure 1.31 appears.
2. Click *light*, then click ▸ to move *light* to the "Variables" box.
3. Click **OK**.

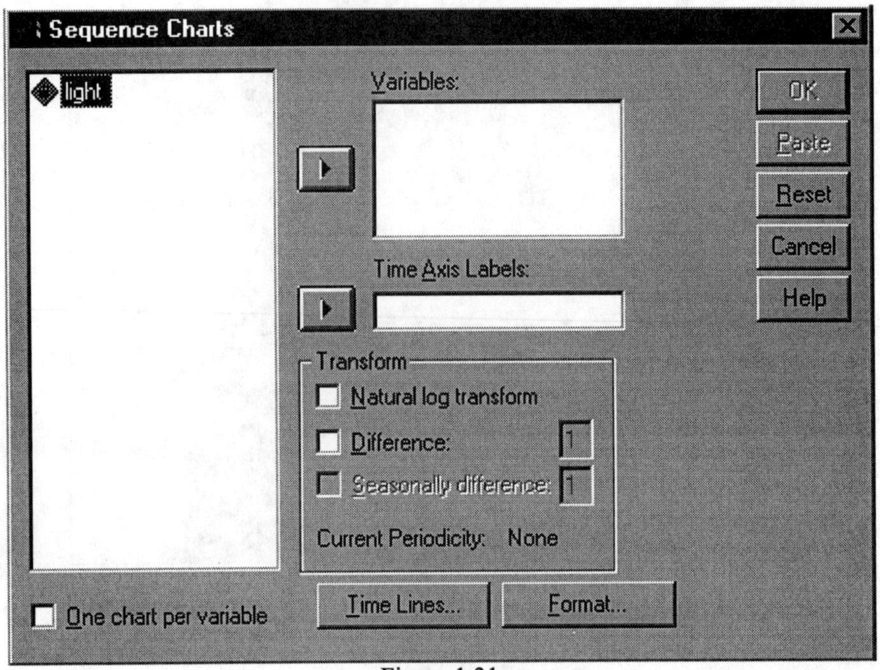

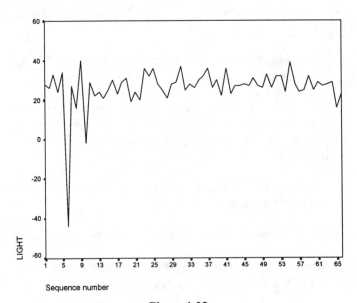

Figure 1.31

Figure 1.32 is the default SPSS output. To change the labels on the *x* axis (also called the category axis in SPSS) and the *y* axis (also called the scale axis in SPSS), consult Example 1.4 and the directions in the Editing Histograms section.

Figure 1.32

Example 1.5
(cont.)

There is some suggestion in this plot that the variability (the vertical spread in the plot) is decreasing over time. In particular, both outlying observations were made early on. Perhaps Newcomb became more adept at using his equipment as he gained experience.

The next example creates a time plot for data that was not only collected yearly but also quarterly.

Example 1.6
(IPS p. 36)

The years around 1970 brought unrest to many U.S. cities. Table 1.7 gives the number of civil disturbances in each three-month period during the years 1968 to 1972.

Make a time plot of these counts.

The SPSS Data Editor contains a single variable called *count*, which is declared type numeric 8.2.

Table 1.7 Number of Civil Disturbances During the Years 1968 – 1972

	Period	Count		Period	Count
1968	Jan.–Mar.	6	1970	July–Sept.	20
	Apr.–June	46		Oct.–Dec	6
	July–Sept.	25	1971	Jan.–Mar.	12
	Oct.–Dec.	3		Apr.–June	21
1969	Jan.–Mar.	5		July–Sept.	5
	Apr.–June	27		Oct.–Dec.	1
	July–Sept.	19	1972	Jan.–Mar.	3
	Oct.–Dec.	6		Apr.–June	8
1970	Jan.–Mar.	26		July–Sept.	5
	Apr.–June	24		Oct.–Dec.	5

To create a date variable for the *x* axis of the time plot, follow these steps.

1. Click **Data** and then click **Define Dates**. The SPSS window in Figure 1.33 appears.

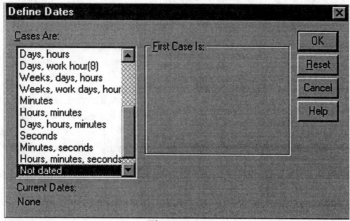

Figure 1.33

43

2. In the "Cases Are" box, click ▲ and then click **Years, quarters** (the appropriate time scale for this example).
3. In the "First Case Is" box, type **1968** (the earliest year) into the "Year" box and **1** into the "Quarter" box.
4. Click **OK**.

Three new variables, called *year_*, *quarter_*, and *date_*, appear in the SPSS Data Editor. The first two observations in the SPSS Data Editor are shown in Table 1.8.

	count	year_	quarter_	date_
1	6.00	1968	1	Q1 1968
2	46.00	1968	2	Q2 1968

Table 1.8

To create a time plot for this data set, follow these steps.

1. Click **Graphs** and then click **Sequence**. The "Sequence Chart" window shown in Figure 1.31 appears with the appropriate variable names in the window.
2. Click *count*, then click ▶ to move *count* to the "Variables" box.
3. Select the desired variable to appear on the *x* axis. Choices include *year_*, *quarter_*, or *date_*. Click the desired variable name (such as *year_*), then click ▶ to move the desired variable (such as *year_*) to the "Time Axis Labels" box.
4. Click **OK**.

Figure 1.34 is the resulting SPSS output (except for selecting the option for the *x* axis to show only "every 4 labels" rather than "all labels", see Figure 1.27). To change the labels on the *x* axis (also called the category axis in SPSS) and *y* axis (also called the scale axis in SPSS), consult Example 1.4 and the directions in the Editing Histograms section.

Example 1.6 (cont.)	The time plot shows seasonal variation, a regular rise and fall that recurs each year, in the number of civil disturbances. The number of civil disturbances is usually highest during the second quarter (April thru June), which represents the spring months.

Section 1.2. Describing Distributions with Numbers

This section introduces the notion of describing distributions with numbers. A description of a distribution almost always includes a **measure of center** and a **measure of spread**. To get a quick summary of both center and spread, use the five-number summary (the **minimum**, the **25ᵗʰ percentile**, the **median**, the **75ᵗʰ percentile**, and the **maximum**). The five-number summary leads to a visual representation of the distribution called a **boxplot**.

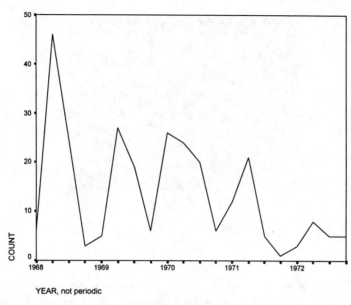

YEAR, not periodic

Figure 1.34

Descriptive Statistics and Boxplots for a Single Quantitative Variable

Example 1.7
(IPS Ex. 1.16)

A marketing consultant observed 50 consecutive shoppers at a supermarket. One variable of interest was how much each shopper spent in the store. See Table 1.4 for the data.

Obtain descriptive statistics and a boxplot for the quantitative variable *spending*.

The SPSS Data Editor contains a single variable called *spending*, which is declared type numeric 8.2.

To obtain descriptive statistics (such as the mean, median, standard deviation, percentiles, etc.) for a quantitative variable, follow these steps.

1. Click **Statistics**, click **Summarize**, and then click **Explore**. The "Explore" window shown in Figure 1.20 appears.
2. Click *spending*, then click ▶ to move *spending* into the "Dependent List" box.
3. By default, the "Display" box in the lower left corner has **Both** selected. Click **Statistics**.
4. Click the **Statistics** button located in lower right corner of the window. The SPSS window in Figure 1.35 appears.
5. Click **Percentiles**. Be sure that a ✔ appears in front of "Descriptives".
6. Click **Continue**.
7. Click **OK**.

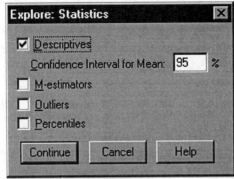

Figure 1.35

Tables 1.9 and 1.10 are the resulting SPSS output.

Descriptives

			Statistic	Std. Error
SPENDING	Mean		34.7022	3.0685
	95% Confidence	Lower Bound	28.5359	
	Interval for Mean	Upper Bound	40.8685	
	5% Trimmed Mean		33.2422	
	Median		27.8550	
	Variance		470.777	
	Std. Deviation		21.6974	
	Minimum		3.11	
	Maximum		93.34	
	Range		90.23	
	Interquartile Range		26.6625	
	Skewness		1.103	.337
	Kurtosis		.709	.662

Table 1.9

Percentiles

		Percentiles						
		5	10	25	50	75	90	95
Weighted	SPENDING	9.0890	12.7990	19.0600	27.8550	45.7225	69.4100	86.0345
Tukey's Hinges	SPENDING			19.2700	27.8550	45.4000		

Table 1.10

Example 1.7 (cont.)   The mean and the median amount spent in the store are $34.70 and $27.86, respectively. The amount of money spent varies from $3.11 to $93.34. The standard deviation is $21.70. SPSS uses slightly different rules than IPS to compute the quartiles, so the results given by the computer may not agree exactly with the results found by using IPS rules. SPSS uses two methods

Example 1.7 (cont.)   (labeled "Weighted" and "Tukey's Hinges" (see Table 1.10)) to calculate the quartiles. The answers between the methods differ slightly ($19.06 versus $19.27 and $45.72 versus $45.40).

To create a boxplot for a quantitative variable, follow these steps.

1.   Click **Graphs** and then click **Boxplot**. The SPSS window in Figure 1.36 appears.

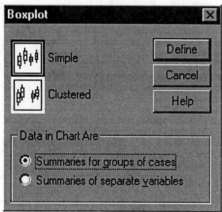

Figure 1.36

2.   Click **Summaries of separate variables** and then click **Define**. The SPSS window in Figure 1.37 appears.

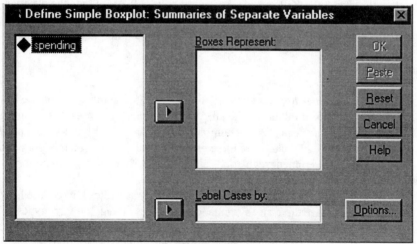

Figure 1.37

3.   Click *spending*, then click ▸ to move *spending* into the "Boxes Represent" box.
4.   Click **OK**.

47

Figure 1.38 is the resulting SPSS output (except for the difference in the color scheme). To change the color or the pattern fill of the boxplot, follow the directions given in Example 1.1 about editing bar charts.

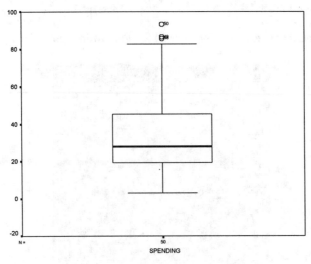

Figure 1.38

Example 1.7 (cont.)

SPSS distinguishes between minor and major outliers. Minor outliers (denoted by ° in the plot) are observations more than $1.5 \times$ IQR outside the central box. Major outliers (denoted by * in the plot) are observations more than $3.0 \times$ IQR outside the central box. SPSS also puts the observation number beside the symbol used for the outlier. For this example, there are three minor outliers occurring at observation numbers 48, 49, and 50.

Comparing Distributions

Example 1.8 (IPS Ex. 1.17)

Consumer Reports (June 1986, pp. 366–367) commented on the low nutritional quality of the all-American frank. The magazine's laboratory test results for calories in a number of major brands of hot dogs are presented in Table 1.11. There are three types: all beef, "meat" (mainly pork and beef, but government regulations allow up to 15% poultry), and poultry.

Because people concerned about health may prefer low-calorie hot dogs, we ask: "Are there any systematic differences among the three types in the variable calories?" We can make the comparison by using some numerical tools and side-by-side boxplots for describing distributions.

The SPSS data editor contains two variables called *type* (declared type string 8) and *calories* (declared type numeric 8.1). The variable *type* contains the following values: beef, meat, or poultry.

48

Table 1.11 Calories in Three Types of Hot Dogs
Beef hot dogs: 186, 181, 176, 149, 184, 190, 158, 139, 175, 148, 152, 111, 141,
                   153, 190, 157, 131, 149, 135, 132
Meat hot dogs: 173, 191, 182, 190, 172, 147, 146, 139, 175, 136, 175, 136, 179,
                   153, 107, 195, 135, 140, 138
Poultry hot dogs: 129, 132, 102, 106, 94, 102, 87, 99, 170, 113, 135, 142, 86, 143,
                   152, 146, 144

To obtain descriptive statistics (such as the mean, median, standard deviation, percentiles, etc.) for a quantitative variable broken down by a categorical variable, follow these steps.

1. Click **Statistics**, click **Summarize**, and then click **Explore**. The "Explore" window shown in Figure 1.20 appears, with the appropriate variable names in the window.
2. Click *calories*, then click ▸ to move *calories* into the "Dependent List" box.
3. Click *type*, then click ▸ to move *type* into the "Factor List" box.
4. By default, the "Display" box in the lower left corner has **Both** selected. Click **Statistics**.
5. Click the **Statistics** button located in lower right corner of window. The "Explore Statistics" window shown in Figure 1.35 appears.
6. Click **Percentiles**. Be sure that "Descriptives" is checked.
7. Click **Continue**.
8. Click **OK**.

Tables 1.12 and 1.13 are part of the resulting SPSS output.

Percentiles

		TYPE	5	10	25	50	75	90	95
Weighted Average(Definition 1)	CALORIES	beef	112.0000	131.1000	139.5000	152.5000	179.7500	189.6000	190.0000
		meat	107.0000	129.4000	138.5000	153.0000	180.5000	191.8000	.
		poultry	86.0000	86.8000	100.5000	129.0000	143.5000	155.6000	.
Tukey's Hinges	CALORIES	beef			140.0000	152.5000	178.5000		
		meat			139.0000	153.0000	179.0000		
		poultry			102.0000	129.0000	143.0000		

Table 1.12

Descriptives

	TYPE			Statistic	Std. Error
CALORIES	beef	Mean		156.8500	5.0629
		95% Confidence Interval for Mean	Lower Bound	146.2532	
			Upper Bound	167.4468	
		5% Trimmed Mean		157.5556	
		Median		152.5000	
		Variance		512.661	
		Std. Deviation		22.6420	
		Minimum		111.00	
		Maximum		190.00	
		Range		79.00	
		Interquartile Range		40.2500	
		Skewness		-.031	.512
		Kurtosis		-.813	.992
	meat	Mean		158.7059	6.1206
		95% Confidence Interval for Mean	Lower Bound	145.7308	
			Upper Bound	171.6809	
		5% Trimmed Mean		159.5621	
		Median		153.0000	
		Variance		636.846	
		Std. Deviation		25.2358	
		Minimum		107.00	
		Maximum		195.00	
		Range		88.00	
		Interquartile Range		42.0000	
		Skewness		-.209	.550
		Kurtosis		-.823	1.063
	poultry	Mean		122.4706	6.1806
		95% Confidence Interval for Mean	Lower Bound	109.3684	
			Upper Bound	135.5728	
		5% Trimmed Mean		121.8562	
		Median		129.0000	
		Variance		649.390	
		Std. Deviation		25.4831	
		Minimum		86.00	
		Maximum		170.00	
		Range		84.00	
		Interquartile Range		43.0000	
		Skewness		.102	.550
		Kurtosis		-1.176	1.063

Table 1.13

To create side-by-side boxplots for a quantitative variable broken down by a categorical variable, follow these steps.

1. Click **Graphs** and then click **Boxplot**. The "Boxplot" window shown in Figure 1.36 appears.
2. Click **Define**. The SPSS window in Figure 1.39 appears.

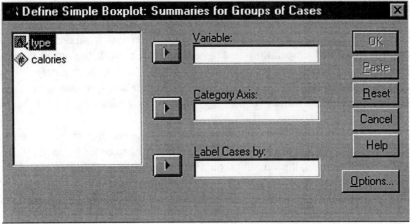

Figure 1.39

3. Click *calories*, then click ▶ to move *calories* into the "Variable" box.
4. Click *type*, then click ▶ to move *type* into the "Category Axis" box.
5. Click **OK**.

Figure 1.40 is the resulting SPSS output (except for the difference in the color scheme). To change the color or the pattern fill of the boxplots, follow the directions given in Example 1.1 about editing bar charts.

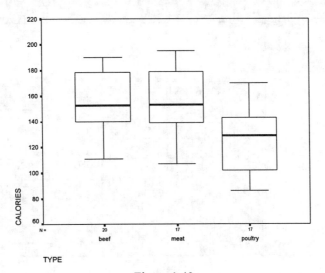

Figure 1.40

Example 1.8
(cont.)

From the side-by-side boxplots, we see at once that poultry franks as a group contain fewer calories than beef or meat hot dogs. The median number of calories in a poultry hot dog is less than the first quartile of either of the other distributions. But each type shows quite a large spread among brands, so simply buying a poultry frank does not guarantee a low-calorie food.

Changing the Unit of Measurement (Linear Transformations)

The same variable can be recorded in different units of measurement. Americans commonly record distances in miles and temperatures in degrees Fahrenheit, while the rest of the world measures distances in kilometers and temperatures in degrees Celsius. Fortunately, it is easy to convert numerical descriptions of a distribution from one unit of measurement to another. This is true because a change in the measurement unit is a **linear transformation** of the measurements.

Example 1.9
(IPS Ex. 1.20)

Suppose you have a data set containing the variable temperature measured in degrees Fahrenheit. In order for the results to be understood by the rest of the world, the variable should be reexpressed in degrees Celsius. The linear transformation is tempcel = (5/9)tempfahr – (160/9), where tempcel = the temperature expressed in degrees Celsius and tempfahr = the temperature expressed in degrees Fahrenheit.

The SPSS Data Editor contains a single quantitative variable called *tempfahr*, which is declared numeric 8.2

To create a new variable in the SPSS Data Editor that is a linear transformation of an existing variable in the SPSS Data Editor, follow these steps.

1. Click **Transform** and then click **Compute**. The SPSS window in Figure 1.41 appears.

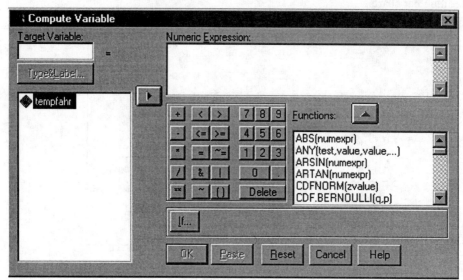

Figure 1.41

2. In the "Target Variable" box, type in *tempcel*.
3. Click *tempfahr*, then click ▸ to move *tempfahr* into the "Numeric Expression" box.
4. In the "Numeric Expression" box, type in the following expression: 5/9*tempfahr – 160/9.
5. Click **OK**. The variable *tempcel* now appears in the "SPSS Data Editor" window.

Section 1.3. Normal Distributions

One particularly important class of density curves is the **normal distribution**. These density curves are symmetric, unimodal, and bell-shaped. All normal distributions have the same overall shape. The exact density curve for a particular normal distribution is specified by giving its mean μ and its standard deviation σ. This section discusses how to use SPSS to do normal distribution probability calculations, how to obtain **normal quantile plots**, and how to generate observations from a normal distribution.

Normal Distribution Probability Calculations

Example 1.10 (IPS Ex. 1.25 and Ex. 1.26)	The level of cholesterol in the blood is important because high cholesterol levels increase the risk of heart disease. The distribution of blood cholesterol levels in a large population of people of the same age and sex is roughly normal. For 14-year-old boys, the mean is 170 milligrams of cholesterol per deciliter of blood (mg/dl) and the standard deviation is 30 mg/dl. Using software, find what proportion of 14-year-old boys have less than 240 mg/dl of cholesterol. What proportion of 14-year-old boys have more than 240 mg/dl of cholesterol? What proportion of 14-year-old boys have blood cholesterol between 170 and 240 mg/dl?

To obtain the proportion of interest, follow these steps.

1. Enter the variables and values of *x1* and *x2* into the SPSS Data Editor, where *x1* = 170 and *x2* = 240.
2. Click **Transform** and then click **Compute**. The "Compute" window shown in Figure 1.41 appears with the exception that *x1* and *x2* appear in the window.
3. In the "Target Variable" box, type in *prop*.
4. In the "Functions" box, click ▾ until **CDF.NORMAL(q, mean, stddev)** appears in the box. Double click on **CDF.NORMAL(q, mean, stddev)** to move **CDF. NORMAL(?, ?, ?)** into the "Numeric Expression" box. The CDF.NORMAL(q, mean, stddev) function stands for the cumulative distribution function for the normal distribution, and it calculates the area to the left of *q* under the correct normal curve.
5. In the "Numeric Expression" box, change the second question mark to **170** and the third question mark to **30** (the appropriate values for the mean and the standard deviation).
6. For the proportion less than 240, **CDF.NORMAL(x2, 170, 30)** should appear in the "Numeric Expression" box. For the proportion more than 240, **1 – CDF.NORMAL(x2, 170, 30)** should appear in the "Numeric Expression" box. For the proportion between 170 and 240, **CDF.NORMAL(x2, 170, 30) – CDF.NORMAL(x1, 170, 30)** should appear in the "Numeric Expression" box.
7. Click **OK**.

The variable *prop* can be found in the SPSS Data Editor. By default, the number of decimal places for the variable *prop* is two. The number of decimal places can be changed; follow the directions given in Section 0.8.

Example 1.10 (cont.)	The proportion of 14-year-old boys with blood cholesterol less than 240 is 0.9902. The proportion of 14-year-old boys with blood cholesterol more than 240 is 0.0098. The proportion of 14-year-olds with blood cholesterol between 170 and 240 is 0.4902.

The previous example showed how to find the relative frequency of a given event. The next example shows how to find the observed value corresponding to a given relative frequency.

Example 1.11 (IPS Ex. 1.27)	Scores on the SAT verbal test in recent years follow approximately a normal distribution with a mean of 505 and a standard deviation of 110. Using software, determine how high a student must score to place in the top 10% of all students taking the SAT.
	After following the steps below, you can see that a student must score at least 646 to place in the top 10% of all students taking the SAT.

To obtain the observed value corresponding to a given relative frequency, follow these steps.

1. Enter the variable and the value of *x1* into the SPSS Data Editor, where *x1* represents the area under the curve to the left of the desired score. Thus, *x1* = 1 – 0.10 = 0.90.
2. Click **Transform** and then click **Compute**. The "Compute" window, shown in Figure 1.41, appears with *x1* in the window.
3. In the "Target Variable" box, type *score*.
4. In the "Functions" box, click ▼ until **IDF.NORMAL(p, mean, stddev)** appears in the box. Double click on **IDF. NORMAL(p, mean, stddev)** to move **IDF. NORMAL(?, ?, ?)** into the "Numeric Expression" box. The IDF.NORMAL(p, mean, stddev) function stands for the inverse of the cumulative distribution function for the normal distribution, and it calculates the X value such that the area to the left of X under the correct normal curve is *p*.
5. In the "Numeric Expression" box, change the first question mark to *x1*, the second question mark to **505** and the third question mark to **110**. Thus, **IDF.NORMAL(x1, 505, 110)** should appear in the "Numeric Expression" box.
6. Click **OK**. The variable *score* can be found in the SPSS Data Editor.

Normal Quantile Plots

A useful tool for assessing normality is a graph called the normal quantile plot. Any data that follow a normal distribution produce a straight line on the normal quantile plot. Systematic deviations from a straight line indicate a nonnormal distribution. Outliers appear as points that are far away from the overall pattern of the plot.

Example 1.12 | Consider Newcomb's light measurement data given in Table 1.6. Assess
(IPS Ex. 1.28) | normality for the distribution by examining the normal quantile plot.

To create a normal Q-Q plot of this distribution, follow these steps.

1. Click **Statistics**, click **Summarize**, and then click **Explore**. The "Explore" window shown in Figure 1.20 appears with the variable *light* in the window.
2. Click *light*, then click ▸ to move *light* into the "Dependent List" box.
3. By default, the "Display" box in the lower left corner has **Both** selected. Click **Plots**.
4. Click **Plots** located next to the "Options" button. The "Explore Plots" window shown in Figure 1.21 appears.
5. Click **None** within the "Boxplots" box.
6. Click **Stem-and-leaf** within the "Descriptive" box. The ✔ disappears.
7. Click **Normality plots with tests**. A ✔ appears in the box.
8. Click **Continue**.
9. Click **OK**.

Figure 1.42 is part of the resulting SPSS output.

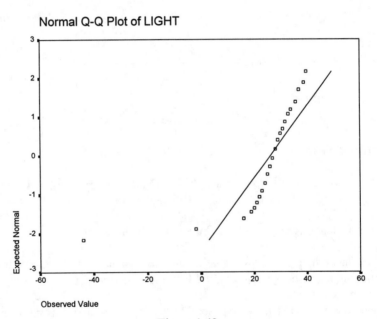

Figure 1.42

Example 1.12 | The points deviate from the straight line, especially the two negative values
(cont.) | of – 2 and – 44, suggesting a nonnormal distribution. The fact that the two lowest values of the passage time of light deviate substantially to the left of the line suggests a left-skewed distribution. This agrees with the histogram shown in Figure 1.30.

Example 1.12 (cont.)   A normal Q-Q plot of Newcomb's data with the two negative values omitted is presented in Figure 1.43. The effect of omitting the outliers is to magnify the plot of the remaining data. Most of the points lie close to the straight line, indicating that a normal model fits well.

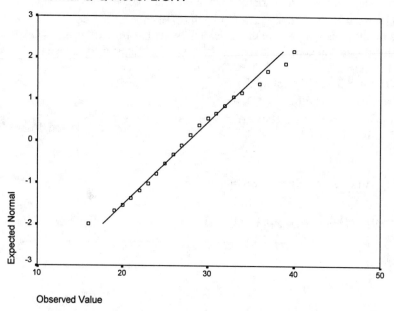

Normal Q-Q Plot of LIGHT

Figure 1.43

Random Number Generator

Example 1.13   Use software to generate 100 observations from a normal distribution with a mean of 25 and a standard deviation of 5.

To generate observations from a normal distribution, follow these steps.

1.   In the SPSS Data Editor, create a variable called *rannorm* that is declared type numeric 8.2 and has 100 missing values (that is, the first 100 cells under the column header *rannorm* should have periods in them).
2.   Click **Transform** and then click **Compute**. The "Compute" window, as shown in Figure 1.41, appears with the appropriate variable names in the window.
3.   In the "Target Variable" box, type in *rannorm*.
4.   In the "Functions" box, click ▼ until **RV.NORMAL(mean, stddev)** appears in the "Functions" box. Double click on **RV. NORMAL(mean, stddev)** to move **RV. NORMAL(?, ?)** into the "Numeric Expression" box.
5.   In the "Numeric Expression" box, change the first question mark to **25** and the second question mark to **5** (the appropriate values for the mean and the standard deviation).
6.   Click **OK**. SPSS asks the question: "Change existing variable?" Click **OK**.

Chapter 2. Looking at Data — Relationships

Section 2.1. Scatterplots, Correlation, and Least Squares Regression

This section introduces analysis of two variables that may have a linear relationship. In analyzing two quantitative variables, it is useful to display the data in a **scatterplot**, determine the **correlation** between the data, and find the **least squares regression** line. A scatterplot is a graph that puts one variable on the x axis and the other on the y axis, and it is used to determine whether an overall pattern exists between the variables. The correlation measures the strength and direction of the linear relationship, and the least squares regression line is the equation of the line that best represents the data.

Example 2.1 **(IPS Ex. 2.11)**	How do children grow? The pattern of growth varies from child to child, so we can best understand the general pattern by following the average height of a number of children. Table 2.1 represents the mean heights of a group of children in Kalama, an Egyptian village that was the site of a study of nutrition in developing countries. The data were obtained by measuring the heights of 161 children from the village each month from 18 to 29 months of age.

Table 2.1 Mean Height of Kalama Children

Age	18	19	20	21	22	23	24	25	26	27	28	29
Mean Height	76.1	77.0	78.1	78.2	78.8	79.7	79.9	81.1	81.2	81.8	82.8	83.5

	Figure 2.1 is the SPSS scatterplot of the data set. Age is the explanatory variable, which is plotted on the x axis. The plot shows a strong, positive, linear association with no outliers. As a result, you might also be interested in obtaining the correlation coefficient and the equation of the regression line.

To generate a scatterplot, follow these steps.

1. Click **Graph**, click **Scatter**, and click **Define**. The "Simple Scatterplot" window in Figure 2.2 appears.
2. Click *age*, then click ▸ to move *age* into the "X Axis" box.
3. Click *height*, then click ▸ to move *height* into the "Y Axis" box.
4. Click **OK**.

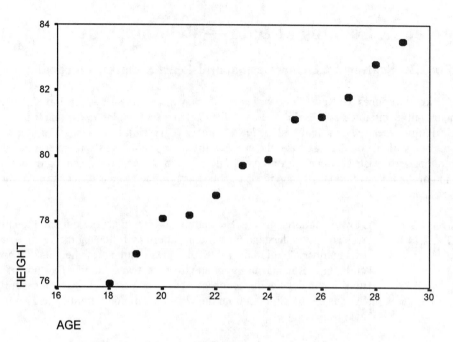

Figure 2.1

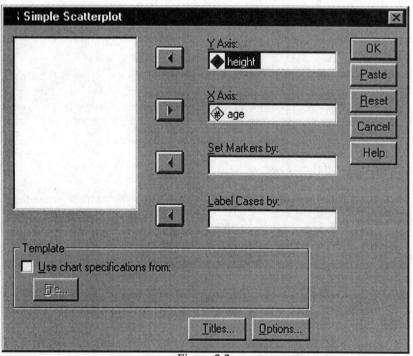

Figure 2.2

To obtain statistics such as the correlation, *y*-intercept, and slope of the regression line, follow these steps.

1. Click **Statistics**, click **Regression**, and then click **Linear**. The "Linear Regression" window in Figure 2.3 appears.
2. Click *age*, then click ▸ to move *age* into the "Independent(s)" box.
3. Click *height*, then click ▸ to move *height* into the "Dependent" box.
4. Click **OK**.

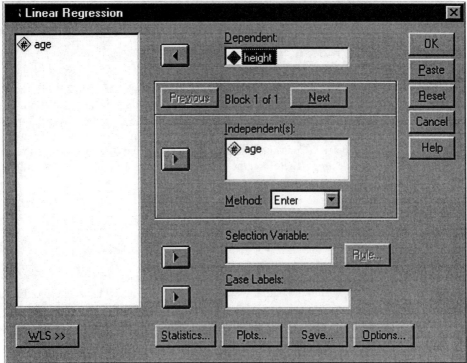

Figure 2.3

Tables 2.2 and 2.3 are part of the SPSS output that shows the correlation, the *y*-intercept, and the slope.

Model Summary

Model	R	R Square	Adjusted R Square	Std. Error of the Estimate
1	.994a	.989	.988	.256

a. Predictors: (Constant), AGE

Table 2.2

Coefficients[a]

Model		Unstandardized Coefficients		Standardized Coefficients	t	Sig.
		B	Std. Error	Beta		
1	(Constant)	64.928	.508		127.709	.000
	AGE	.635	.021	.994	29.665	.000

a. Dependent Variable: HEIGHT

Table 2.3

Example 2.1 (cont.)

The correlation is $r = 0.994$, and $r^2 = 0.989$, found in Table 2.2. The value of r confirms that these data have a strong, positive, linear association. The intercept is $a = 64.928$, and the slope is $b = 0.635$, found in Table 2.3 in the "Unstandardized Coefficients" column. The y-intercept is the value in the row labeled "(Constant)", and the slope is denoted by its variable name, in this case, *age*. Therefore, the equation of the least squares regression line is

$$\hat{y} = 64.928 + 0.635x.$$

To plot the least squares regression line on the scatterplot, follow these steps.

1. Generate the scatterplot as described at the beginning of this chapter.
2. When the scatterplot appears in the output window, double click inside the scatterplot to gain access to the Chart Editor.
3. Once in the Chart Editor, click **Chart**, click **Options**, and then click **Total**, which is found in the "Fit Line" box (see Figure 2.4).
4. Click **Fit Options**. The window in Figure 2.5 appears.
5. The "Fit Method" defaults to "Linear regression," which is what is desired.
6. If you are interested in displaying R^2 in the legend of the scatterplot, click **Display R-square in legend**.
7. Click **Continue**.
8. Click **OK**.

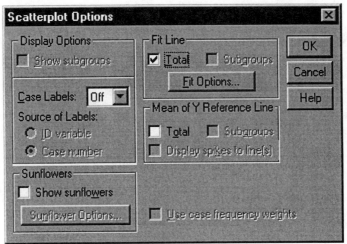

Figure 2.4

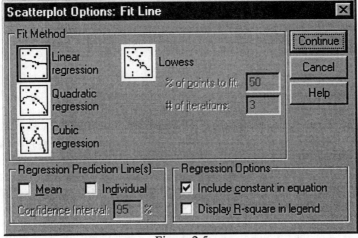

Figure 2.5

Example 2.1 (cont.)

Figure 2.6 is the least squares regression line plotted on the scatterplot of the Kalama children data set. Recall that the equation of the line is $\hat{y} = 64.928 + 0.635x$, and the correlation is $r = 0.994$. Such a high correlation indicates that the linear relationship is indeed very strong, and the relationship is confirmed by the way the points cluster around the least squares regression line in Figure 2.6.

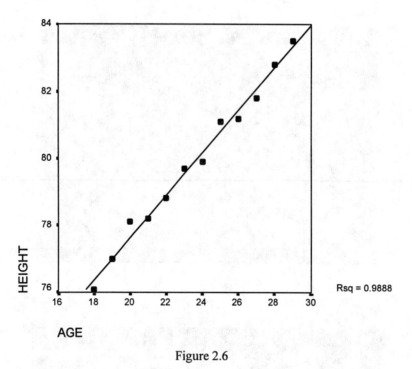

Figure 2.6

Section 2.2. Residuals

A **residual** is the difference between an observed value of the response variable and the value predicted by the regression line, written $residual = y - \hat{y}$. The primary purpose for analyzing residuals is to determine whether the linear model best represents a data set. **Residual plots** are a type of scatterplot in which the independent variable is often on the x axis and the residuals are on the y axis. This type of plot is used to detect patterns that may exist by magnifying the deviations from the line. It is desirable for no pattern to exist on the residual plot, but instead for the plot to be an unstructured band centered around $y = 0$. If this is the case, then a linear fit is appropriate. If a pattern does exist on the residual plot, it could indicate that the relationship between y and x is nonlinear or that perhaps the variation of y is not constant as x increases. Residual plots are also useful in identifying outliers and influential observations.

To generate the residuals, follow these steps.

1. Click **Statistics**, click **Regression**, and then click **Linear**.
2. Click *age*, then click ‣ to move *age* into the "Independent(s)" box.
3. Click *height*, then click ‣ to move *height* into the "Dependent" box.
4. Click **Save**, then click **Unstandardized** which is found in the "Residuals" box (see Figure 2.7).
5. Click **Continue**, then **OK**.

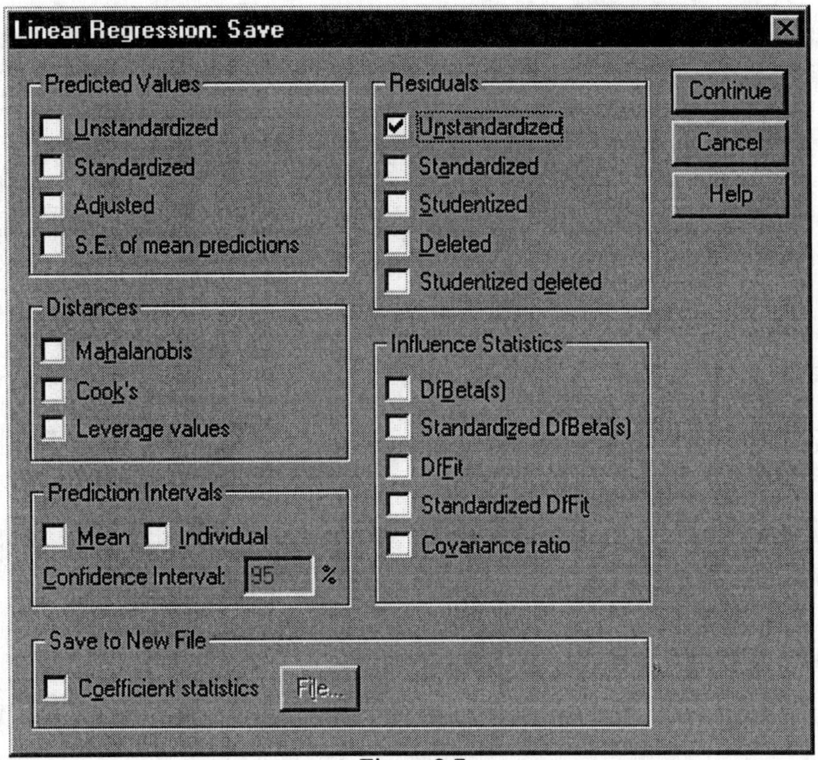

Figure 2.7

The residuals for this data set have been generated, saved, and added to the Data Editor, as shown in Figure 2.8.

To plot the residuals against the independent variable, in this case, *age*, and to plot the reference line at $y = 0$ on this plot, follow these steps.

1. Click **Graph**, click **Scatter**, and then click **Define**.
2. Click *age*, then click ▸ to move *age* into the "X Axis" box.
3. Click *Unstandardized Residuals (res_1)*, then click ▸ to move *Unstandardized Residuals (res_1)* into the "Y Axis" box.
4. Click **OK**.
5. When the scatterplot appears in the output window, double click inside the scatterplot to gain access to the Chart Editor.
6. Click **Chart**, click **Reference Line**, and then click **Y scale** (see Figure 2.9). This places a horizontal reference line that crosses the *y* axis.

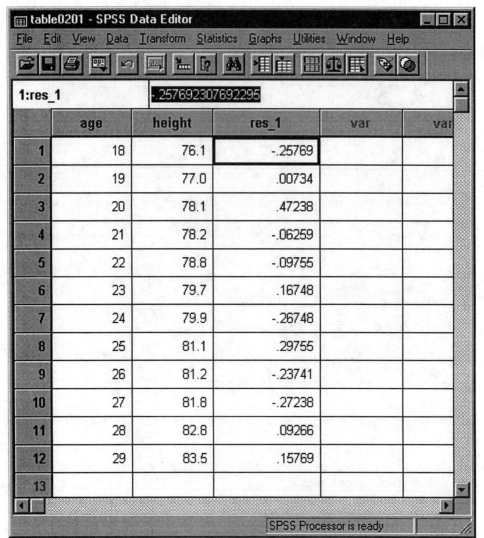

Figure 2.8

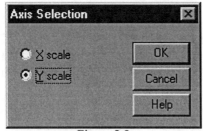

Figure 2.9

7. Click **OK**. The "Scale Axis Reference Lines" window in Figure 2.10 appears.
8. Since a horizontal line at $y = 0$ is desirable, and the field entitled "Position of Line(s)" defaults at 0, click **Add**.
9. Click **OK**. The resulting plot is in Figure 2.11.

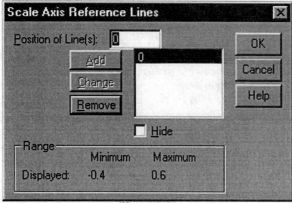

Figure 2.10

Example 2.1 (cont.) Note how the residuals of the Kalama data in Figure 2.11 are randomly scattered around the line $y = 0$. This indicates that the linear model is an appropriate model for this data set.

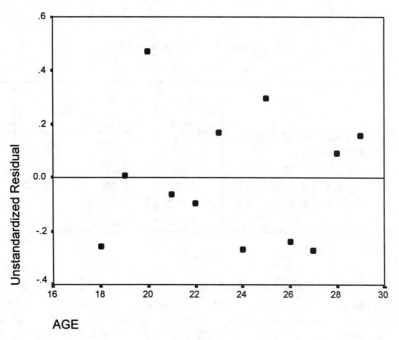

Figure 2.11

SPSS has the capability to perform more advanced regression diagnostics, such as DFFITS (difference between fitted values), studentized residuals, and other techniques. To get to the SPSS window that produces the data necessary for such techniques, follow the instructions presented earlier for generating the residuals. Please refer to Figure 2.7, the SPSS window "Linear Regression: Save". The diagnostic statistics are in the box entitled "Influence Statistics".

Section 2.3. Relations in Categorical Data

This section focuses on how to describe **relationships** between two or more categorical variables. To analyze **categorical data**, we use counts (frequencies) or percents (relative frequencies) of individuals that fall into various categories.

**Example 2.2
(IPS Ex. 2.28)**

Table 2.4 presents Census Bureau data on the years of school completed by Americans of different ages. Many people under 25 years of age have not completed their education, so they are left out of the table. Both variables, age and education, are grouped into categories. This is a two-way table because it describes two categorical variables. Education is the row variable because each horizontal row in the table describes people with one level of education. Age is the column variable because each vertical column describes one age group. The entries in the table are the counts of persons in each age-by-education class. Although both age and education in this table are categorical variables, both have a natural order from least to most. The order of the rows and columns in Table 2.4 reflects the order of the categories. The values given in Table 2.4 are in thousands of persons (e.g., there were 30,512,000 persons who did not complete high school).

ED_LEVEL * AGE Crosstabulation

Count

		AGE			
		25 to 34	35 to 54	55 and over	Total
ED_LEVEL	Did not complete high school	5325	9152	16035	30512
	Completed high school	14061	24070	18320	56451
	College, 1 to 3 years	11659	19926	9662	41247
	College, 4 or more years	10342	19878	8005	38225
Total		41387	73026	52022	166435

Table 2.4

Note: The values in Table 2.4 of this manual were generated using the cell counts from Table 2.14 in IPS. If you compare the marginal totals in Table 2.4 of this manual with Table 2.14 in IPS, you will notice a few discrepancies. For example, the sum of the entries in the "25 to 34" column in Table 2.4 of this manual is 41,387 whereas the entry for that column in Table 2.14 in IPS is 41,388. The explanation is roundoff error. The table entries are in thousands of persons, and each is rounded to the nearest thousand. The Census Bureau obtained the "Total" entry by rounding the exact number of people aged 25 to 34 to the nearest thousand. The result was 41,388,000. Adding the row entries, each of which is already rounded, gives a slightly different result. This explains why some values that add up in Table 2.4 of this manual do not add up in Table 2.14 in IPS.

Example 2.2 (cont.)

Figure 2.12 shows how the data were entered in SPSS. The variables of *age*, *ed_level*, and *weight* were all declared numeric of length 8.0. Note that the values of 1, 2, and 3 were used to represent the values of "25 to 34", "35 to 54", and "55 and over", respectively, for the variable *age*. Similarly, the values of 1, 2, 3, and 4 were used to represent the values of "Did not complete high school", "Completed high school", "College, 1 to 3 years", "College, 4 or more years", respectively, for the variable *ed_level*. The values were matched (e.g., 1 = "25 to 34") using the **labels** option under **define variable** (see Section 0.8).

age	ed_level	weight
1	1	5325
1	2	14061
1	3	11659
1	4	10342
2	1	9152
2	2	24070
2	3	19926
2	4	19878
3	1	16035
3	2	18320
3	3	9662
3	4	8005

Figure 2.12

Prior to generating Table 2.4, you must first weight cases since summary information is being used. For instance, the 8th data row in Figure 2.12 represents 19,878(000) individuals who had the characteristics of being in the 35 to 54 age group (value 2 with the variable *age*) and who completed 4 or more years of college (value 4 with the variable *ed_level*). If the weighting option were not used, it would take 19,878 rows of data (*age* =1, *ed_level* = 1) to represent the same information. In fact, if the weighting

**Example 2.2
(cont.)**

option were not used, it would take 166,438 rows to completely represent the information. Instead, by using the weighting option, we can represent the entire data in only 12 rows.

To activate the weighting option, follow these steps.

1. Click **Data**, and click **Weight Cases**. The "Weight Cases" window in Figure 2.13 appears.

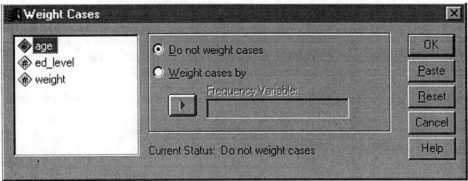

Figure 2.13

2. Click **Weight cases by**.
3. Click *weight*, then click ▸ to move *weight* into the "Frequency Variable" box.
4. Click **OK**.

Now that the weighting option has been activated, you can generate Table 2.4 by following these steps.

1. Click **Statistics**, click **Summarize**, and then click **Crosstabs**. The "Crosstabs" window in Figure 2.14 appears.
2. Click *ed_level*, then click ▸ to move *ed_level* into the "Row(s)" box.
3. Click *age*, then click ▸ to move *age* into the "Column(s)" box.
4. Click **OK**.

If you want to compare the conditional distributions of education within the three age groups, follow these steps.

1. Click **Statistics**, click **Summarize**, and then click **Crosstabs**. The SPSS window in Figure 2.14 appears.
2. Click *ed_level*, then click ▸ to move *ed_level* into the "Row(s)" box.
3. Click *age*, then click ▸ to move *age* into the "Column(s)" box.
4. Click the **Cells** button. Click **Column** in the "Percentages" box (since age is the column variable being conditioned on), then click **Continue**.
5. Click **OK**.

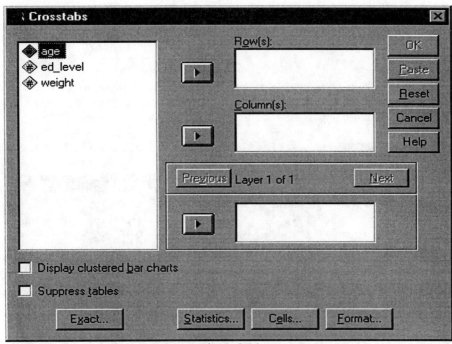

Figure 2.14

Table 2.5 shows the resulting SPSS output.

ED_LEVEL * AGE Crosstabulation

			AGE			
			25 to 34	35 to 54	55 and over	Total
ED_LEVEL	Did not complete high school	Count	5325	9152	16035	30512
		% within AGE	12.9%	12.5%	30.8%	18.3%
	Completed high school	Count	14061	24070	18320	56451
		% within AGE	34.0%	33.0%	35.2%	33.9%
	College, 1 to 3 years	Count	11659	19926	9662	41247
		% within AGE	28.2%	27.3%	18.6%	24.8%
	College, 4 or more years	Count	10342	19878	8005	38225
		% within AGE	25.0%	27.2%	15.4%	23.0%
Total		Count	41387	73026	52022	166435
		% within AGE	100.0%	100.0%	100.0%	100.0%

Table 2.5

Example 2.2 (cont.) Information about the 25 to 34 age group is contained in the first column of Table 2.5. Given that a person is 25 to 34 years of age, the conditional distribution of education is 12.9% for "Did not complete high school", 34.0% for "Completed high school", 28.2% for "College, 1 to 3 years", and

Example 2.2 (cont.) 25.0% for "College, 4 or more years". The conditional distributions of education, given that a person is 35 to 54 years of age and 55 years of age and over, are displayed in columns two and three of Table 2.5, respectively.

Bar graphs can help make the conditional distribution more apparent. If you are interested in obtaining a bar graph showing the conditional distribution of education given that a person is 24 to 34 years of age, follow these steps.

1. Click **Data**, and click **Select Cases**. The "Select Cases" window in Figure 2.15 appears.

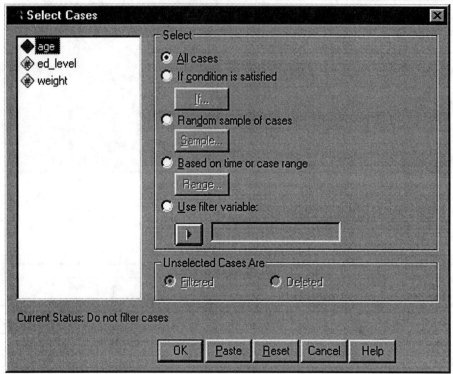

Figure 2.15

2. Click **If condition is satisfied**, then click **If**.
3. Click *age*, then click ▶ to move *age* into the upper right box.
4. Click =, then click **1**. The upper right box should now read as shown in Figure 2.16.
5. Click **Continue**, then click **OK**.

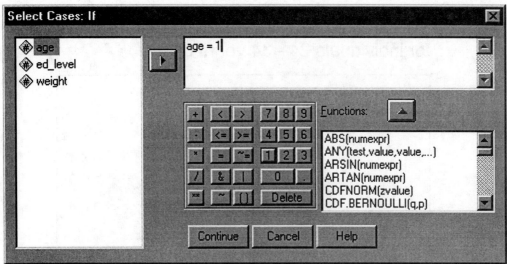

Figure 2.16

6. A new variable, *filter_$*, appears in the SPSS Data Editor. All cases that have a value of 1 for *age* also have a value of 1 for *filter_$* (indicating that these cases were selected). In addition, all cases that have a value of 2 or 3 for *age* have a value of 0 for *filter_$* (indicating that these cases were not selected). Further, cases that have a value other than 1 for *age* now have an off-diagonal line through the observation indicating that these cases will be excluded from any subsequent analyses.

7. Click **Graphs**, then click **Bar**. By default, SPSS assumes that you want a simple bar chart and that the data in the charts represent summaries for groups of cases. Since both of these are appropriate for this example, click **Define**.

8. Click *edlevel*, then click ▸ to move *edlevel* into the "Category Axis" box.

9. Click **% of cases** under the "Bars Represent" box.

10. Click **Titles** and type **Conditional distribution of education** in the "Line 1" box under Title, press the **Tab** key, and type **for individuals 24 – 34 years of age** in the "Line 2" box under Title.

11. Click **Continue**, then click **OK**. The bar chart shown in Figure 2.17 appears (after changing the color of the bar chart and adding percent values to the bars).

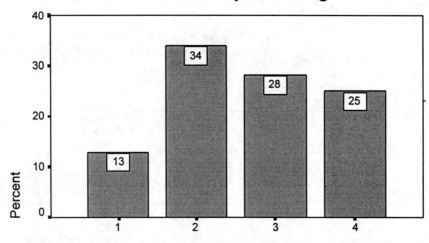

Conditional distribution of education
for individuals 24 - 34 years of age

ED_LEVEL

Cases weighted by WEIGHT

Figure 2.17

**Example 2.2
(cont.)**

As Figure 2.17 suggests, of the people 25 to 34 years of age, approximately 13% did not complete high school, 34.0% completed high school, 28% completed 1 to 3 years of college, and 25.0% completed 4 or more years of college. These numbers agree with column one in Table 2.5.

Chapter 3. Producing Data

This chapter demonstrates how SPSS can be used to **select *n* cases** from a finite population of interest using **simple random sampling**. Simple random sampling, the most basic sampling design, allows impersonal chance to choose the cases for inclusion in the sample, thus eliminating bias in the selection procedure.

Example 3.1
(IPS Ex. 3.16)

An academic department wishes to choose a three-member advisory committee at random from the 28 faculty members of the department who are listed in Table 3.1.

Table 3.1 Faculty Names

00	Abbott	07	Goodwin	14	Pillotte	21	Theobald
01	Cicirelli	08	Haglund	15	Raman	22	Vader
02	Cuellar	09	Johnson	16	Riemann	23	Wang
03	Dunsmore	10	Keegan	17	Rodriguez	24	Wieczorek
04	Engle	11	Luo	18	Rowe	25	Williams
05	Fitzpatrick	12	Martinez	19	Sommers	26	Wilson
06	Garcia	13	Nguyen	20	Stone	27	Wong

One option is to use a table of random digits. Another option is to use SPSS to randomly choose 3 of the 28 faculty members. A data file was created using the variable *name* (declared as a string variable with length 12), which contained the names of the 28 faculty members of the department.

To select a random sample of *n* cases from *N* cases, follow these steps.

1. Click **Data,** and click **Select Cases**. The "Select Cases" window in Figure 3.1 appears.
2. Click **Random sample of cases** and then click the **Sample** button. The "Select Cases: Random Sample" window in Figure 3.2 appears.
3. Click **Exactly □ cases from the first □ cases** and fill in the boxes so that the line reads "Exactly **3** cases from the first **28** cases".
4. Click **Continue**.
5. Click **OK**.

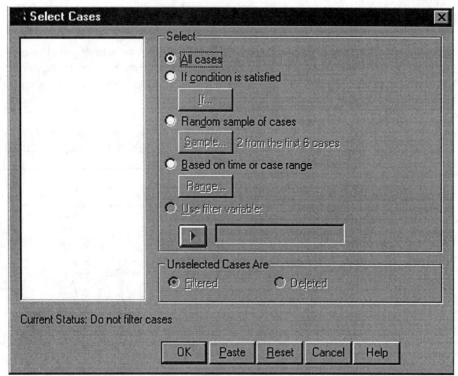

Figure 3.1

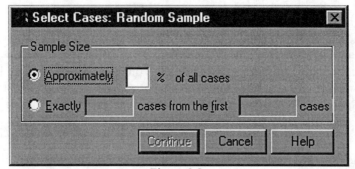

Figure 3.2

**Example 3.1
(cont.)**

SPSS creates a new variable, *filter_$*, which is assigned a value of 0 if the case was not randomly selected and a value of 1 if the case was randomly selected. Further, unselected cases are marked in the Data Editor with a diagonal line through the row number, as can be seen in Figure 3.3, which shows the first 10 cases. With this procedure, faculty members Abbott, Rowe, and Wieczorek were randomly selected to serve on the advisory committee. If the *filter_$* variable is deleted and the procedure repeated, a different set of faculty members should be randomly selected to serve.

	name	filter_$
1	Abbott	1
2	Cicirelli	0
3	Cuellar	0
4	Dunsmore	0
5	Engle	0
6	Fitzpatrick	0
7	Garcia	0
8	Goodwin	0
9	Haglund	0
10	Johnson	0

Figure 3.3

Chapter 4. Probability Distributions

This chapter will show how SPSS can be used to find **probabilities** associated with both **binomial** and **normal probability distributions**. In addition, a list of other probability distributions for which SPSS can calculate probabilities is given at the end of the chapter.

Section 4.1. Binomial Probability Distributions

Example 4.1
(IPS Ex. 5.4)
A quality control engineer selects a simple random sample of 10 switches from a large shipment for detailed inspection. Unknown to the engineer, 10% of the switches in the shipment fail to meet the specifications. What is the probability that no more than 1 of the 10 switches in the sample fails inspection?

Let X = the number of switches in the sample that fail to meet the specifications. X is a binomial random variable with $n = 10$ and $p = 0.10$. To find the probability that no more than 1 of the 10 switches in the sample fails inspection (P(X ≤ 1 | $n = 10$, $p = 0.10$), follow these steps.

1. Define a new variable *switch*, which takes on the values 0 through 10. This variable is declared a numeric variable of length 8.0.
2. Click **Transform** and then click **Compute**. The "Compute Variable" window in Figure 4.1 appears.

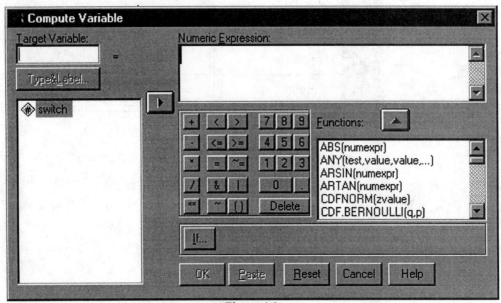

Figure 4.1

3. In the "Target Variable" box, type in *lesseq*.
4. In the "Functions" box, click ▼ until **CDF.BINOM(q,n,p)** appears in the box. Double click

on **CDF.BINOM(q,n,p)** to move CDF.BINOM(?,?,?) into the "Numeric Expression" box. The CDF.BINOM(q,n,p) function stands for the cumulative distribution function for the binomial distribution, and it calculates the cumulative probability that the variable takes a value less than or equal to q.

5. In the "Numeric Expression" box, highlight the first *?*, click on *switch*, and click ▸ so that *switch* replaces the first *?*. Delete the second *?* and replace it with the number **10** (the value of *n*), and delete the third *?* and replace it with the value **0.10** (the value of *p*).
6. Click **OK**.

Figure 4.2 displays the new variable *lesseq*. By default, SPSS shows the values of *lesseq* to two decimal places of accuracy. The number of decimal places was changed to four (see Section 0.8).

switch	lesseq
0	.3487
1	.7361
2	.9298
3	.9872
4	.9984
5	.9999
6	1.0000
7	1.0000
8	1.0000
9	1.0000
10	1.0000

Figure 4.2

For each value of *switch*, the variable *lesseq* represents the cumulative probability of observing that number or fewer failures.

Example 4.1 (cont.) We want to determine the probability that no more the 1 of the 10 switches in the sample fails inspection or, symbolically, $P(X \leq 1 \mid n = 10, p = 0.10)$. The variable *lesseq* tells us that the probability that no more than 1 of the 10 switches in the sample fails inspection is 0.7361, given the probability that any given switch will fail is $p = 0.10$.

Example 4.1 (cont.)

Given the same values of n and p, suppose we want to find the probability that strictly less than two switches fail inspection ($P(X < 2 \mid n = 10, p = 0.10)$). Steps 2 – 6 can be repeated with the changes that the target variable is named *less* and the "Numeric Expression" box reads **CDF.BINOM(switch–1,10,0.10)**. If we want to determine the probability that exactly two of the 10 switches fail inspection ($P(X = 2 \mid n = 10, p = 0.10)$), steps 2 – 6 can be repeated with the changes that the target variable is named *equal* and the "Numeric Expression" box reads **CDF.BINOM(switch,10,0.10) – CDF.BINOM(switch–1,10,0.10)**. If we want to determine the probability that at least two of the 10 switches fail inspection ($P(X \geq 2 \mid n = 10, p = 0.10)$), steps 2 – 6 can be repeated with the changes that the target variable is named *greateq* and the "Numeric Expression" box reads **1 – CDF.BINOM(switch–1,10,0.10)**. Last, if we want to determine the probability that strictly more than two of the 10 switches fail inspection ($P(X > 2 \mid n = 10, p = 0.10)$), steps 2 – 6 can be repeated with the changes that the target variable is named *greater* and the "Numeric Expression" box reads **1 – CDF(switch,10,0.10)**. The probabilities associated with $X \leq 2$, $X < 2$, $X = 2$, $X \geq 2$, and $X > 2$ are shown in Figure 4.3 under the variables of *lesseq*, *less*, *equal*, *greateq*, and *greater*, respectively. All five of these variables were changed so that they show four decimal places of accuracy (see Section 0.8).

switch	lesseq	less	equal	greateq	greater
2	.9298	.7361	.1937	.2639	.0702

Figure 4.3

Section 4.2. Normal Probability Distributions

Example 4.2

The level of cholesterol in the blood is important because high cholesterol levels increase the risk of heart disease. The distribution of blood cholesterol levels in a large population of people of the same age and sex is roughly normal. For 14-year-old boys, the mean is 170 milligrams of cholesterol per deciliter of blood (mg/dl) and the standard deviation is 30 mg/dl. Using software and the normal distribution, find the approximate probability that a randomly selected 14-year-old boy has a cholesterol level less than 240 mg/dl. Find the approximate probability that a randomly selected 14-year-old boy has a cholesterol level of more than 240 mg/dl of cholesterol. Find the approximate probability that a randomly selected 14-year-old boy has a cholesterol level between 170 and 240 mg/dl.

Let X = the cholesterol level of a randomly selected 14-year-old boy. X is approximately N(170,30). To find the probabilities, follow the directions given in Example 1.10.

Example 4.2 (cont.) The approximate probability that a randomly selected 14-year-old boy has a cholesterol level less than 240 mg/dl is 0.9902. The approximate probability that a randomly selected 14-year-old boy has a blood cholesterol level more than 240 is 0.0098. The approximate probability that a randomly selected 14-year-old boy has a cholesterol level between 170 and 240 is 0.4902.

Section 4.3. Other Probability Distributions

SPSS is capable of computing probabilities for a number of distributions. Table 4.1 displays a number of commonly used distributions and their commands.

Table 4.1

Distribution	SPSS Command
Chi-square	CDF.CHISQ(q,df)
Exponential	CDF.EXP(q,scale)
F	CDF.F(q,df1,df2)
Geometric	CDF.GEOM(q,p)
Hypergeometric	CDF.HYPER(q,total,sample,hits)
Poisson	CDF.POISSON(q,mean)
Uniform	CDF.UNIFORM(q,min,max)

Chapter 5. Sampling Distributions

A probability distribution for a sample statistic is often referred to as a **sampling distribution**. This chapter describes how to simulate random samples from a known population and compute sample statistics for the generated samples. The generated samples can then be utilized to examine properties of sampling distributions.

Section 5.1. Generating Binomial Data

Example 5.1 (IPS Ex. 5.9) | A national opinion poll found that 44% of all American adults agree that parents should be given vouchers good for education at any public or private school of their choice. Suppose that, in fact, 44% of the population feel this way. A study is conducted that surveys the opinion of 100 American adults. Simulation will be used to examine properties of the sampling distribution for the proportions.

To simulate 500 replications of 100 surveys, follow these steps.

1. Click **File**, click **New**, and then click **Syntax**. The SPSS Syntax Editor in Figure 5.1 (without the text) appears.
2. Type the program appearing in Figure 5.1 into the Syntax Editor.

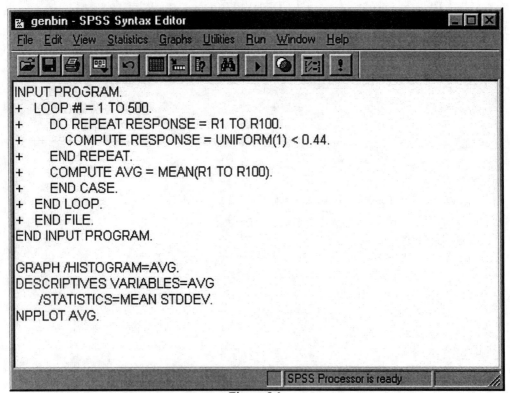

```
genbin - SPSS Syntax Editor
File  Edit  View  Statistics  Graphs  Utilities  Run  Window  Help

INPUT PROGRAM.
+   LOOP # = 1 TO 500.
+      DO REPEAT RESPONSE = R1 TO R100.
+         COMPUTE RESPONSE = UNIFORM(1) < 0.44.
+      END REPEAT.
+      COMPUTE AVG = MEAN(R1 TO R100).
+      END CASE.
+   END LOOP.
+   END FILE.
END INPUT PROGRAM.

GRAPH /HISTOGRAM=AVG.
DESCRIPTIVES VARIABLES=AVG
     /STATISTICS=MEAN STDDEV.
NPPLOT AVG.

                                          SPSS Processor is ready
```

Figure 5.1

3.   To run the program, click **Run**, then click **All**.

The SPSS output in Figure 5.2 and Table 5.1 displays the resulting histogram and table of descriptive statistics for a particular simulation. Note that another simulation will produce different results.

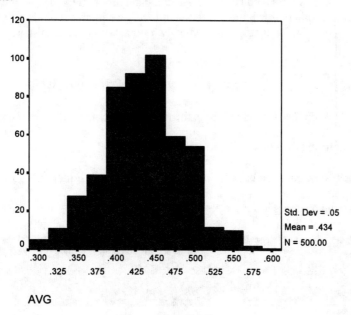

Figure 5.2

Descriptive Statistics

	N	Mean	Std. Deviation
AVG	500	.4342	5.057E-02
Valid N (listwise)	500		

Table 5.1

Example 5.1 (cont.)   By the Central Limit Theorem the sampling distribution for the sample proportion in this example is approximately normal with mean and standard deviation of

$$\mu_{\hat{p}} = 0.44 \text{ and } \sigma_{\hat{p}} = \sqrt{(0.44)(0.56)/100} = 0.0496.$$

The results of the simulation are consistent with the theoretical results.

81

Section 5.2. Generating Normal Data

Example 5.2
(IPS Ex. 5.14)

The height of a randomly selected young woman follows a normal distribution with a mean of 64.5 inches and a standard deviation of 2.5 inches. If a medical study asked the height of 100 young women, the sampling distribution of the sample mean height would have a sampling distribution that is approximately normal with mean and standard deviation of

$$\mu_{\bar{x}} = 64.5 \text{ and } \sigma_{\bar{x}} = 2.5/\sqrt{100} = 0.25.$$

A simulation that confirms the theoretical results will be demonstrated.

To simulate 1000 replications of this study, follow these steps.

1. Click **File**, click **New**, and then click **Syntax**. The SPSS Syntax Editor in Figure 5.3 (without the text) appears.
2. Type the program appearing in Figure 5.3 into the Syntax Editor.

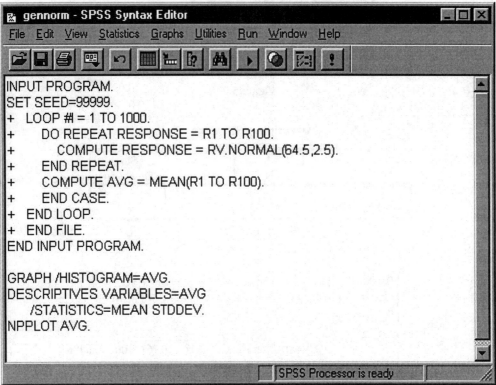

```
INPUT PROGRAM.
SET SEED=99999.
+    LOOP # = 1 TO 1000.
+        DO REPEAT RESPONSE = R1 TO R100.
+            COMPUTE RESPONSE = RV.NORMAL(64.5,2.5).
+        END REPEAT.
+        COMPUTE AVG = MEAN(R1 TO R100).
+        END CASE.
+    END LOOP.
+    END FILE.
END INPUT PROGRAM.

GRAPH /HISTOGRAM=AVG.
DESCRIPTIVES VARIABLES=AVG
    /STATISTICS=MEAN STDDEV.
NPPLOT AVG.
```

Figure 5.3

3. To run the program, click **Run**, then click **All**.

The resulting SPSS output contains the histogram, descriptive statistics, and normal Q-Q plot appearing in Figure 5.4, Table 5.2, and Figure 5.5, respectively.

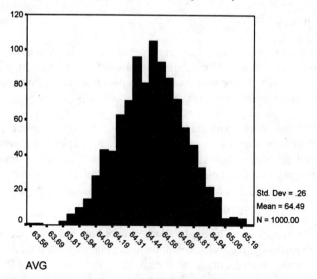

Figure 5.4

Descriptive Statistics

	N	Mean	Std. Deviation
AVG	1000	64.4888	.2564
Valid N (listwise)	1000		

Table 5.2

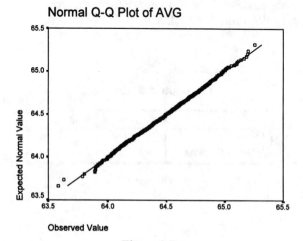

Figure 5.5

83

Chapter 6. Introduction to Inference

Section 6.1. Confidence Intervals

A **confidence interval** is a procedure for estimating a population parameter using observed data, and a **test of significance** is a procedure for determining the validity of a claim using observed data. This chapter describes how to **simulate** random samples from a known population and examine various properties of confidence intervals and tests of significance.

Example 6.1 **(IPS Ex. 5.14)**	The height of a randomly selected young woman follows a normal distribution with a mean of 64.5 inches and a standard deviation of 2.5 inches. If a medical study asked the height of 25 young women, the data might be used to estimate the mean height of young women. Assuming that $\sigma = 2.5$, a 90% confidence interval for the mean height is given by $$\bar{x} \pm 1.645\left(2.5/\sqrt{25}\right).$$ A simulation can be used to demonstrate how a confidence interval works. Specifically, the following simulation generates 1000 random samples of 25. For each sample, the mean is computed, and the resulting 90% confidence interval is constructed. The program then determines whether each confidence interval contains the true mean of 64.5. After the 1000 replications, the simulation tabulates the percentage of confidence intervals that contain the true mean. Table 6.1 displays the percentage of confidence intervals in the simulation that contain the true mean. The observed percentage of confidence intervals that contain the true mean of 64.5 is 89.4%.

To simulate 1000 replications of 25 samples, follow these steps.

1. Click **File**, click **New**, and then click **Syntax**. The SPSS Syntax Editor in Figure 6.1 (without the text) appears.
2. Type the program appearing in Figure 6.1 into the Syntax Editor.
3. To run the program, click **Run**, then click **All**.

Descriptive Statistics

	N	Mean
INSIDE	1000	.8940
Valid N (listwise)	1000	

Table 6.1

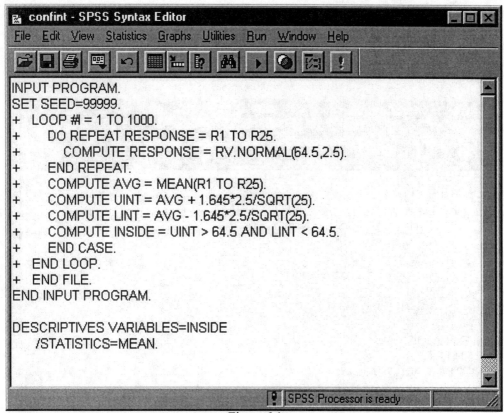

```
confint - SPSS Syntax Editor                        _ □ X

File  Edit  View  Statistics  Graphs  Utilities  Run  Window  Help

INPUT PROGRAM.
SET SEED=99999.
+   LOOP # = 1 TO 1000.
+      DO REPEAT RESPONSE = R1 TO R25.
+         COMPUTE RESPONSE = RV.NORMAL(64.5,2.5).
+      END REPEAT.
+      COMPUTE AVG = MEAN(R1 TO R25).
+      COMPUTE UINT = AVG + 1.645*2.5/SQRT(25).
+      COMPUTE LINT = AVG - 1.645*2.5/SQRT(25).
+      COMPUTE INSIDE = UINT > 64.5 AND LINT < 64.5.
+      END CASE.
+   END LOOP.
+   END FILE.
END INPUT PROGRAM.


DESCRIPTIVES VARIABLES=INSIDE
    /STATISTICS=MEAN.

                              ⚡ SPSS Processor is ready
```

Figure 6.1

Section 6.2. Tests of Significance

Example 6.2
(IPS Ex. 6.16)

Bottles of a popular cola drink are supposed to contain 300 milliliters (ml) of cola, although there is always inherent variation from bottle to bottle because the filling machinery is not precise. The distribution of the contents is normal with standard deviation $\sigma = 3$ ml. A student who suspects that the bottler is underfilling measures the contents of six bottles and tests the hypotheses H_0: $\mu = 300$ and H_a: $\mu < 300$ at the 5% significance level.

A simulation can be used to demonstrate how a test of significance works. Specifically, the following simulation generates 1000 random samples of 6. For each sample, the mean is computed, and the resulting test statistic is determined. The program then determines whether each test statistic is less than the critical value of -1.645. After the 1000 replications the simulation tabulates the percentage of test statistics that are less than the critical value of -1.645.

To simulate 1000 replications of 6 samples, follow these steps.

1. Click **File**, click **New**, and then click **Syntax**. The SPSS Syntax Editor in Figure 6.2 (without the text) appears.
2. Type the program appearing in Figure 6.2 into the Syntax Editor.

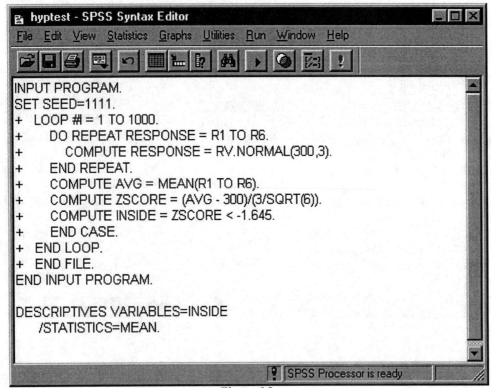

Figure 6.2

3. To run the program, click **Run**, then click **All**.

Table 6.2 displays the percentage of test statistics that are less than the critical value of −1.645.

Descriptive Statistics

	N	Mean
INSIDE	1000	4.800E-02
Valid N (listwise)	1000	

Table 6.2

Example 6.2
(cont.)

The observed significance level for the simulation was 0.048, which is consistent with the significance level of 0.05. In addition, a simulation can be used to examine the power of the test against the specific alternative of μ = 297. The test rejects H_o when the test statistic z is less than -1.645 or when the sample mean $\bar{x}$ is less than 297.985. Then the power is

$$P(\bar{x} \leq 297.985) = P\left(z \leq \frac{297.985 - 297}{3/\sqrt{6}}\right) = P(z \leq 0.8045) = 0.7894.$$

The previous program can be used to simulate the observed power by generating samples with a mean of 297. This is accomplished by generating a RESPONSE = RV.NORMAL(297,3) rather than a RESPONSE = RV.NORMAL(300,3). Table 6.3 displays the results of the revised simulation. The observed power for the simulation was 0.7840, which is consistent with the power of the test against the specific alternative of μ = 297.

Descriptive Statistics

	N	Mean
INSIDE	1000	.7840
Valid N (listwise)	1000	

Table 6.3

Chapter 7. Inference for Distributions

Section 7.1. Inference for the Mean of a Population

This section introduces the use of the *t* **distribution** in inferential statistics for the mean of a population. When σ is unknown for the population, the *t* distribution, rather than the *z* distribution, is used. A particular *t* distribution is specified by giving the degrees of freedom. The **one-sample *t* confidence interval for** μ (the population mean), the **one-sample *t* test for** μ, the **matched pairs *t* procedures**, and the **sign test** (a distribution-free procedure) are discussed in this section.

One-Sample *t* Confidence Interval

Example 7.1 **(IPS Ex. 7.4)**	The first reasonably accurate measurements of the speed of light were made over 100 years ago by Simon Newcomb between July and September 1882. See Example 1.4 for details of the data set (given in Table 1.6). Compute a 99% confidence interval for μ where μ is the mean of the distribution of measurements from which Newcomb's 64 measurements are a sample. Before proceeding with the confidence interval for the mean, we must verify the assumption of normally distributed data. A normal quantile plot (see Example 1.12) reminds us that when the outliers to the left (– 44 and – 2) are omitted, the remaining 64 observations follow a normal distribution quite closely. The SPSS Data Editor contains a single variable called *light*, which is declared type numeric 8.2.

To obtain a confidence interval for μ, follow these steps.

1. Click **Statistics**, click **Summarize**, and then click **Explore**. The SPSS window in Figure 7.1 appears.
2. Click *light*, then click ▸ to move *light* into the "Dependent List" box.
3. By default, a 95% confidence interval for μ will be computed. To change the confidence level, click **Statistics**. The "Explore Statistics" window shown in Figure 1.35 appears. Change 95 to **99** in the "Confidence Interval for Mean" box. Click **Continue**.
4. By default, the "Display" box in the lower left corner of the "Explore" window has "Both" selected. Click **Statistics**.
5. Click **OK**.

Table 7.1 contains the resulting SPSS output.

> We are 99% confident that the mean of the distribution of measurements from which Newcomb's 64 measurements are a sample lies somewhere between 26.0622 and 29.4378.

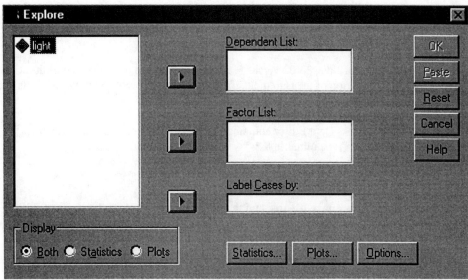

Figure 7.1

Descriptives

			Statistic	Std. Error
LIGHT	Mean		27.7500	.6354
	99% Confidence	Lower Bound	26.0622	
	Interval for Mean	Upper Bound	29.4378	
	5% Trimmed Mean		27.7396	
	Median		27.5000	
	Variance		25.841	
	Std. Deviation		5.0834	
	Minimum		16.00	
	Maximum		40.00	
	Range		24.00	
	Interquartile Range		6.7500	
	Skewness		.154	.299
	Kurtosis		.150	.590

Table 7.1

One-Sample *t* Test

**Example 7.2
(IPS Ex. 7.5)**   The best modern measurements of the speed of light correspond to a passage
time of 33.02 in Newcomb's experiment. Is Newcomb's result significantly
different from this modern value at $\alpha=0.01$? See Example 1.4 for details of
the data set (given in Table 1.6). Before proceeding with the one-sample *t*
test, we must verify the assumption of normally distributed data. A normal

89

Example 7.2 (cont.)

quantile plot (see Example 1.12) reminds us that when the outliers to the left (– 44 and – 2) are omitted, the remaining 64 observations follow a normal distribution quite closely.

Set up H_0: $\mu = 33.02$ versus H_a: $\mu \neq 33.02$, where μ = the mean of the distribution of measurements from which Newcomb's 64 measurements are a sample.

The SPSS Data Editor contains a single variable called *light*, which is declared type numeric 8.2.

To conduct a one-sample *t* test, follow these steps.

1. Click **Statistics**, click **Compare Means**, and then click **One-Sample T Test**. The SPSS window in Figure 7.2 appears.

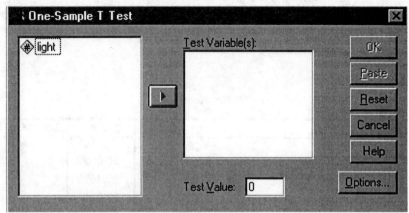

Figure 7.2

2. Click *light*, then click ▶ to move *light* to the "Test Variable(s)" box.
3. Change 0 in the "Test Value" box to **33.02** (the value of μ under H_0).
4. By default, a 95% confidence interval for μ will be part of the one-sample *t* test output. To change the confidence level, click **Options**, change 95 to **99** in the "Confidence Interval" box, and then click **Continue**.
5. Click **OK**.

Table 7.2 is part of the resulting SPSS output.

Example 7.2 (cont.)

The *P*-value of 0.000 is under the Sig. (2-tailed) column. This does not mean that the *P*-value is zero; it means that the *P*-value is less than 0.001. To view more significant digits for the *P*-value, double click on the One Sample Test table in the "Output1 – SPSS Viewer" window and then double click on **.000**. The *P*-value is 1.53×10^{-12}. We can safely reject H_0 in favor of H_a; that is, there is sufficient evidence at the 0.01 level to conclude that the mean of the distribution of measurements from which Newcomb's 64 measurements are a sample is different from 33.02. In addition, we are 99% confident that the true mean of the measurements minus 33.02 lies

90

Example 7.2
(cont.)

between -6.9578 and -3.5822. This answer is consistent with Example 7.1 since $-6.9578 + 33.02 = 26.0622$ and $-3.5822 + 33.02 = 29.4378$, the two endpoints of the 99% confidence interval for μ.

One-Sample Test

	t	df	Sig. (2-tailed)	Mean Difference	99% Confidence Interval of the Difference	
					Lower	Upper
LIGHT	-8.294	63	.000	-5.2700	-6.9578	-3.5822

The header "Test Value = 33.02" spans the t, df, Sig., Mean Difference, and 99% Confidence Interval columns.

Table 7.2

Example 7.3

The one-sample t statistic for testing H_0: $\mu = 10$ versus one of the following, H_a: $\mu < 10$, H_a: $\mu > 10$, or H_a: $\mu \neq 10$, from a sample of $n = 23$ observations has the value $t = 2.78$. Using software, find the exact P-value.

To obtain the P-value, follow these steps.

1. Enter the value of the test statistic into the SPSS Data Editor under the variable called ***teststat***.
2. Click **Transform** and then click **Compute**. The SPSS window in Figure 7.3 appears.

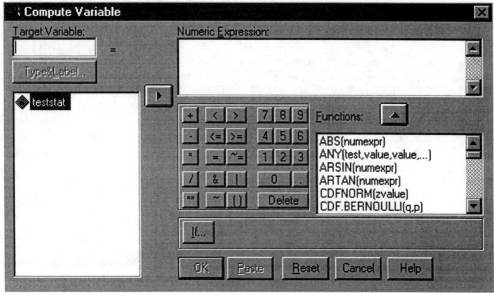

Figure 7.3

3. In the "Target Variable" box, type in ***pvalue***.

4. In the "Functions" box, click ▾ until **CDF.T(q,df)** appears in the "Functions" box. Double click on **CDF.T(q,df)** to move **CDF.T(?,?)** into the "Numeric Expression" box. The CDF.T(q,df) function stands for the cumulative distribution function for the t distribution, and it calculates the area to the left of q under the correct t distribution.

5. In the "Numeric Expression" box, change the first ? to *teststat* and the second ? to **22** (23 − 1). For H_a: $\mu < 10$, **CDF.T(*teststat*,22)** should appear in the "Numeric Expression" box. For H_a: $\mu > 10$, **1 − CDF.T(*teststat*,22)** should appear in the "Numeric Expression" box. For H_a: $\mu \neq 10$, **2*(1 − CDF.T(ABS(*teststat*,22)))** should appear in the "Numeric Expression" box.

6. Click **OK**.

Example 7.3 (cont.)	The *P*-value can be found in the SPSS Data Editor. By default, the number of decimal places for the variable *pvalue* is two. The number of digits after the decimal place can be changed by following the directions in Section 0.8. The *P*-value for H_a: $\mu < 10$ is 0.995. The *P*-value for H_a: $\mu > 10$ is 0.005. The *P*-value for H_a: $\mu \neq 10$ is 0.011.

Matched Pairs *t* Procedure

Example 7.4 (IPS Ex. 7.7)	The National Endowment for the Humanities sponsors summer institutes to improve the skills of high school teachers of foreign languages. One such institute hosted 20 French teachers for 4 weeks. At the beginning of the period, the teachers were given the Modern Language Association's listening test of understanding of spoken French. After 4 weeks of immersion in French in and out of class, the listening test was given again. (The actual French spoken in the two tests was different, so that simply taking the first test should not have improve the score on the second test.) The maximum possible score on the test is 36. Assess whether the institute significantly improved the teachers' comprehension of spoken French at the $\alpha = 0.10$. The data are given in Table 7.3.

Table 7.3 Modern Language Association Listening Scores for French Teachers

Teacher	Pretest	Posttest	Gain	Teacher	Pretest	Posttest	Gain
1	32	34	2	11	30	36	6
2	31	31	0	12	20	26	6
3	29	35	6	13	24	27	3
4	10	16	6	14	24	24	0
5	30	33	3	15	31	32	1
6	33	36	3	16	30	31	1
7	22	24	2	17	15	15	0
8	25	28	3	18	32	34	2
9	32	26	-6	19	23	26	3
10	20	26	6	20	23	26	3

This example is a **matched pairs study**, where before-and-after observations on the same subjects were obtained. To obtain the SPSS output presented in this example (especially the matched pairs *t* test output), the posttest score was the first variable in the SPSS data set and the pretest score was the second variable, where both variables were declared numeric 8.2. Before proceeding with the matched pairs *t* test, we must verify the

Example 7.4 (cont.) | assumption that the differences (the *gain* variable in Table 7.3, which equals *posttest – pretest*) come from a normal distribution. If the variable *gain* has not been entered into the original SPSS data set, the variable *gain* must be created to check the assumption of normality.

To create the variable *gain*, follow these steps.

1. Click **Transform** and then click **Compute**. The SPSS window in Figure 7.3 appears, with *posttest* and *pretest* in the window.
2. In the "Target Variable" box, type *gain*.
3. Double click *posttest*, click the gray minus sign (–), double click *pretest*, and then *posttest – pretest* appears in the "Numeric Expression" box.
4. Click **OK**. The variable *gain* appears in the SPSS data set.

Example 7.4 (cont.) | To obtain the normal quantile plot for the variable *gain*, see the directions given in Example 1.12. Even though the normal quantile plot displays an outlier at – 6, the overall pattern of the plot is otherwise roughly straight. For this reason, the matched pairs *t* test will be applied to all the data and then the results will be compared to the results from the matched pairs *t* test that was applied to the data with the outlier of – 6 removed.

Set up H_0: $\mu = 0$ versus H_a: $\mu > 0$, where μ = the mean improvement (posttest – pretest) that would be achieved if the entire population of French teachers attended a summer institute.

To conduct a matched pairs *t* test, follow these steps.

1. Click **Statistics**, click **Compare Means**, and then click **Paired-Samples T Test**. The SPSS window in Figure 7.4 appears.

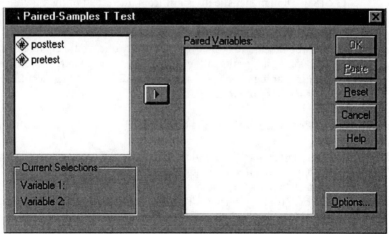

Figure 7.4

2. Click *posttest*. The variable *posttest* appears after "Variable 1" in the "Current Selections" box.
3. Click *pretest*. The variable *pretest* appears after "Variable 2" in the "Current Selections" box.

4. Click ▸. Then *posttest – pretest* appears in the "Paired Variables" box.
5. By default, a 95% confidence interval for μ will be part of the matched pairs *t* test output. To change the confidence level, click **Options**, change 95 to **90** in the "Confidence Interval" box, and then click **Continue**.
6. Click **OK**.

Table 7.4 is part of the resulting SPSS output.

Paired Samples Test

		Paired Differences							
					90% Confidence Interval of the Difference				
		Mean	Std. Deviation	Std. Error Mean	Lower	Upper	t	df	Sig. (2-tailed)
Pair 1	POSTTEST - PRETE	2.5000	2.8928	.6469	1.3815	3.6185	3.865	19	.001

Table 7.4

The same results would have been obtained if we had applied the one-sample *t* test to the variable *gain* using a test value of 0 (follow the directions given in Example 7.2).

Example 7.4 (cont.)

Because of the one-sided alternative, we are only interested in the upper right tail above 3.865. Therefore, the *P*-value is 0.0005. This is obtained by taking the value under the Sig. (2-tailed) column and dividing it by 2 (0.001/2). We can safely reject H_0 in favor of H_a, that is, there is sufficient evidence at the 0.10 level to conclude that the mean improvement that would be achieved if the entire population of French teachers attended a summer institute is greater than 0. In addition, we are 90% confident that the mean improvement that would be achieved if the entire population of French teachers attended a summer institute lies somewhere between 1.3815 and 3.6185. Though statistically significant, the effect of the institute was rather small.

If we drop the single outlier of – 6, the *P*-value would change from 0.0005 to 0.0000058. The results of the *t* procedure with the outlier are conservative in the sense that the conclusions show a smaller effect than would be the case if the outlier was not present.

Inference for Nonnormal Populations Using the Sign Test

Example 7.5 (IPS Ex. 7.12)

Return to the data of Example 7.4 showing the improvement in French listening scores after attending a summer institute. In that example we used the matched pairs *t* test on these data, despite an outlier that makes the *P*-value only roughly correct. The sign test is based on the following simple observation: of the 17 teachers whose scores changed, 16 improved and only 1 did worse. The sign test is a distribution-free procedure designed to cope with nonnormal data. The distribution-free test does not ask the same question (Has the mean changed?) that the *t* test asks. Set up $H_0: p = \frac{1}{2}$ versus $H_a: p > \frac{1}{2}$, where p = the probability that a randomly chosen

**Example 7.5
(cont.)**

teacher would improve if she attended the institute. The *P*-value calculation is based on the binomial distribution rather than the *t* distribution.

To obtain the SPSS output presented in this example, the posttest score was the first variable in the SPSS data set and the pretest score was the second variable, where both variables were declared numeric 8.2.

To perform the sign test, follow these steps.

1. Click **Statistics**, click **Nonparametric Tests**, and then click **2 Related Samples**. The SPSS window in Figure 7.5 appears.

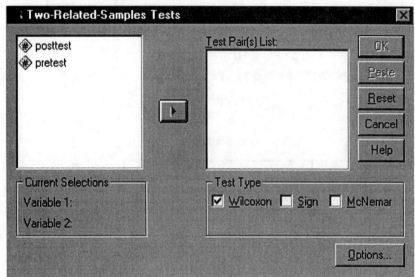

Figure 7.5

2. Click *posttest*. The variable *posttest* appears after "Variable 1" in the "Current Selections" box.
3. Click *pretest*. The variable *pretest* appears after "Variable 2" in the "Current Selections" box.
4. Click ▸ . Then *posttest – pretest* appears in the "Test Pair(s) List" box.
5. Click **Wilcoxon** in the "Test Type" box. The ✓ in front of "Wilcoxon" disappears.
6. Click **Sign** in the "Test Type" box. A ✓ appears in front of "Sign".
7. Click **OK**.

Tables 7.5 and 7.6 are the resulting SPSS output. Although posttest – pretest had appeared in the "Test Pair(s)List" box, SPSS gives output involving pretest – posttest. The output states that the negative and positive differences are 16 and 1, respectively, for pretest – posttest. Thus, the negative and positive differences would be 1 and 16, respectively, for posttest – pretest. However, the two-tailed *P*-value (located in the Exact Sig. (2-tailed) value box) is the same whether pretest – posttest or posttest – pretest is used.

**Example 7.5
(cont.)**

The Exact Sig. (2-tailed) value box contains the *P*-value for H_a: $p \neq \frac{1}{2}$. The value of 0.000 does not mean that the two-tailed *P*-value is zero; it means that the two-tailed *P*-value is less than 0.001. Because of the one-sided

Example 7.5 (cont.)

alternative, we can safely say that the P-value is less than 0.0005 (0.001/2). Therefore, we can reject H_0 in favor of H_a; that is, there is sufficient evidence at the 0.10 level to conclude that the probability that a randomly chosen teacher would improve if she attended the institute is greater than 1/2.

Frequencies

		N
PRETEST - POSTTEST	Negative Differences[a]	16
	Positive Differences[b]	1
	Ties[c]	3
	Total	20

a. PRETEST < POSTTEST

b. PRETEST > POSTTEST

c. POSTTEST = PRETEST

Table 7.5

Test Statistics[b]

	PRETEST - POSTTEST
Exact Sig. (2-tailed)	.000[a]

a. Binomial distribution used.

b. Sign Test

Table 7.6

Section 7.2. The Two-Sample t Procedures

This section introduces the use of the t distribution in inferential statistics for comparing two means. The two-sample problem examined in this section compares the responses in the two groups, where the responses in each group are independent of those in the other group. Assuming the two samples come from normal populations, the **two-sample t procedure** is the correct test to apply.

Example 7.6 (IPS Ex. 7.17)

The pesticide DDT causes tremors and convulsions if it is ingested by humans or other mammals. Researchers seek to understand how the convulsions are caused. In a randomized comparative experiment, 6 white rats poisoned with DDT were compared with a control group of 6 unpoisoned rats. Electrical measurements of nerve activity are the main clue to the nature of DDT poisoning. When a nerve is stimulated, its electrical response shows a sharp spike followed by a much smaller second spike. Researchers found that the second spike is larger in rats fed DDT than in normal rats. This observation helps biologists understand how DDT causes tremors. The researchers measured the amplitude of the second spike as a percentage of the first spike when a nerve in the rat's leg was stimulated. Is

Example 7.6
(cont.)

there sufficient evidence at the 0.05 level to conclude that the population means differ between the two groups? The data for the 12 rats are given in Table 7.7.

Table 7.7 DDT versus Control

Rat	Group	Spike	Rat	Group	Spike
1	DDT	12.207	7	CONTROL	11.074
2	DDT	16.869	8	CONTROL	9.686
3	DDT	25.050	9	CONTROL	12.064
4	DDT	22.429	10	CONTROL	9.351
5	DDT	8.456	11	CONTROL	8.182
6	DDT	20.589	12	CONTROL	6.642

Before proceeding with the two-sample t test, we must verify that the assumptions of normally distributed data in both groups is reasonably satisfied. Both populations are reasonably normal (which can be determined using normal quantile plots for the two groups of data; see directions in Example 1.12), as far as can be judged from six observations.

Set up H_0: $\mu_1 = \mu_2$ versus H_a: $\mu_1 \neq \mu_2$, where μ_1 = the true mean percentage of the amplitude of the second spike compared to the first spike in the DDT group and μ_2 = the true mean percentage of the amplitude of the second spike compared to the first spike in the control group. The SPSS Data Editor contains the variables *group* (declared type string 8) and *spike* (declared numeric 8.3).

To perform the two-sample t test, follow these steps.

1. Click **Statistics**, click **Compare Means**, and then click **Independent-Samples T Test**. The SPSS window in Figure 7.6 appears.
2. Click *spike*, then click ▶ to move *spike* into the "Test Variable(s)" box.

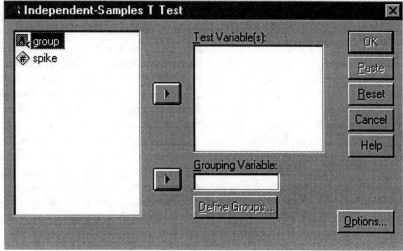

Figure 7.6

3. Click *group*, then click ▶ to move *group* into the "Grouping Variable" box.
4. Click **Define Groups**. The SPSS window in Figure 7.7 appears.

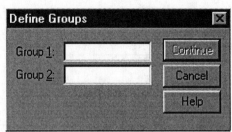

Figure 7.7

5. Type *DDT* in the "Group 1" box. Press the tab key. Type *CONTROL* in the "Group 2" box. Note: The groups must be defined exactly as they appear in the SPSS Data Editor. Click **Continue. Group('DDT' 'CONTROL')** appears in the "Grouping Variable" box.
6. By default, a 95% confidence interval for $\mu_1 - \mu_2$ (the difference in population means) will be part of the two-sample *t* test output. To change the confidence level, click **Options**, change 95 to the desired confidence level in the "Confidence Interval" box, and then click **Continue**.
7. Click **OK**.

Table 7.8 is part of the resulting SPSS output.

Independent Samples Test

		Levene's Test for Equality of Variances		t-test for Equality of Means						95% Confidence Interval of the Difference	
		F	Sig.	t	df	Sig. (2-tailed)	Mean Difference	Std. Error Difference		Lower	Upper
SPIKE	Equal variances assumed	7.658	.020	2.991	10	.014	8.10017	2.70802		2.06632	14.13401
	Equal variances not assumed			2.991	5.938	.025	8.10017	2.70802		1.45697	14.74336

Table 7.8

Example 7.6 (cont.)

SPSS reports the results of two *t* procedures: the pooled two-sample *t* procedure (assumes equal population variances) and a general two-sample *t* procedure (does not assume equal population variances). To determine which *t* procedure to use, SPSS performs Levene's Test for Equality of Variances for H_0: $\sigma_1^2 = \sigma_2^2$ versus H_a: $\sigma_1^2 \neq \sigma_2^2$. The F test statistic for the Levene's test is obtained by computing a one-way analysis of variance (see Chapter 12) on the absolute deviations of each case from its group mean. The P-value for Levene's test of 0.020 is located under the Sig. column. We reject H_0 in favor of H_a, that is, there is sufficient evidence at the 0.05 level to conclude that the population variances are unequal. Thus, we use the two-sample *t* procedure for which equal variances are not assumed. The P-value for the appropriate two-sample *t* procedure is 0.025 (found under the Sig. (2-tailed) column). We reject H_0 in favor of H_a; that is, there is sufficient evidence at the 0.05 level to conclude that the population means differ between the two groups. In addition, we are 95% confident that $\mu_1 - \mu_2$ lies somewhere between 1.45697 and 14.74336.

Chapter 8. Inference for Proportions

This chapter in IPS focuses on inference about population proportions. The first section in this chapter addresses inference on a single population proportion, and the second section addresses comparing two population proportions. Although SPSS programs could be written to perform inference for proportions, it is the our opinion that the analyses discussed in this chapter can be better accomplished using a calculator or another statistical package. It should be noted that after the test statistic is computed for a test of significance, SPSS can be used to easily compute the P-value for the test as described in Example 7.3 of Section 7.1. Note that the problems in this chapter utilize the z distribution. As a result, the P-values would be computed using the function CDF.NORMAL(q,0,1), as described in Example 1.10 of Section 1.3.

Chapter 9. Inference for Two-Way Tables

This chapter introduces the notion of analyzing two categorical variables. The data are often summarized using a **two-way table** (see Section 2.3). **Inferential** procedures are applied to test whether the two categorical variables are independent.

**Example 9.1
(IPS Ex. 9.3)**

Do men and women participate in sports for the same reasons? One goal for sports participants is social comparison — the desire to win or to do better than other people. Another is mastery — the desire to improve one's skills or to try one's best. A study on why students participate in sports collected data from 67 male and 67 female undergraduates at a large university. Each student was classified into one of four categories based on his or her responses to a questionnaire about sports goals. The four categories were high social comparison-high mastery (HSC-HM), high social comparison-low mastery (HSC-LM), low social comparison-high mastery (LSC-HM), and low social comparison-low mastery (LSC-LM). One purpose of the study was to compare the goals of male and female students. The data are displayed in a two-way table (Table 9.1).

Table 9.1 Counts of Goal by Gender

	Observed Counts for Sports Goal		
	Gender		
Goal	Female	Male	Total
HSC-HM	14	31	45
HSC-LM	7	18	25
LSC-HM	21	5	26
LSC-LM	25	13	38
Total	67	67	134

The entries in this table are the observed, or sample, counts. For example, there are 14 females in the high social comparison-high mastery group. Note that the marginal totals are given with the table. They are not part of the raw data but are calculated by summing the rows or columns. The column totals are the numbers of observations sampled in the two populations. The grand total, 134, can be obtained by summing the row or the column totals. It is the total number of observations in the study.

Note: These data were entered using the three variables *gender*, *goal*, and *weight*, where *weight* represents the count for a particular combination of *gender* and *goal*. Prior to any analyses, the **Weight Cases** option under **Data** was activated (see Example 2.2 in Chapter 2 for a reference on how to enter data from a contingency table and how to activate the weighting option).

To describe the relationship between these two categorical variables, percents can generated and compared. Each cell count can be expressed as a percent of the grand total, the row total, and the column total. To generate these percents, follow these steps.

1. Click **Statistics**, click **Summarize**, and then click **Crosstabs**. The "Crosstabs" window in Figure 9.1 appears.

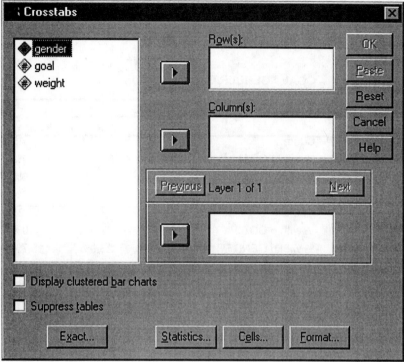

Figure 9.1

2. Click *goal*, then click ▸ to move *goal* into the "Row(s)" box.
3. Click *gender*, then click ▸ to move *gender* into the "Column(s)" box.
4. Click the **Cells** button. The "Crosstabs: Cell Display" window in Figure 9.2 appears.

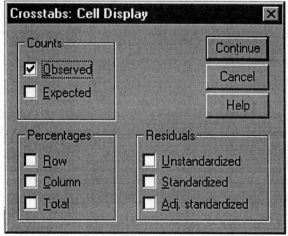

Figure 9.2

5. Click **Row**, **Column**, and **Total** within the "Percentages" box so that a check mark (✔) appears before each type of percentage.
6. Click **Continue**.
7. Click **OK**.

The resulting SPSS output is shown in Table 9.2.

GOAL * GENDER Crosstabulation

			GENDER		
			Female	Male	Total
GOAL	HSC-HM	Count	14	31	45
		% within GOAL	31.1%	68.9%	100.0%
		% within GENDER	20.9%	46.3%	33.6%
		% of Total	10.4%	23.1%	33.6%
	HSC-LM	Count	7	18	25
		% within GOAL	28.0%	72.0%	100.0%
		% within GENDER	10.4%	26.9%	18.7%
		% of Total	5.2%	13.4%	18.7%
	LSC-HM	Count	21	5	26
		% within GOAL	80.8%	19.2%	100.0%
		% within GENDER	31.3%	7.5%	19.4%
		% of Total	15.7%	3.7%	19.4%
	LSC-LM	Count	25	13	38
		% within GOAL	65.8%	34.2%	100.0%
		% within GENDER	37.3%	19.4%	28.4%
		% of Total	18.7%	9.7%	28.4%
Total		Count	67	67	134
		% within GOAL	50.0%	50.0%	100.0%
		% within GENDER	100.0%	100.0%	100.0%
		% of Total	50.0%	50.0%	100.0%

Table 9.2

Example 9.1 (cont.)

Each cell contains four entries, which are labeled at the beginning of each row. The "Count" is the cell count. The "% within GOAL" is the cell count expressed as a percent relative to the row total. As an example, out of all 45 individuals who were classified as HSC-HM, 14, or 13.1%, were female. The "% within GENDER" is the cell count expressed as a percent relative to the column total. For instance, out of the 67 males, 5, or 7.5%, were classified as LSC-HM. The "% of Total" is the cell count expressed as a percent relative to the grand total. Of the 134 total individuals who participated in the study, 25, or 18.7%, were females classified as LSC-LM.

**Example 9.1
(cont.)**

In this example, we are most interested in the effect of gender on the distribution of sports goals. As such, to compare the genders, the column percents or the percents within gender are examined. A higher percent of males were classified as HSC, regardless of the level of mastery, whereas a higher percent of females were classified as LSC, regardless of the level of mastery. This suggests that females and males have different goals when they participate in recreational sports.

The differences between the distribution of males and females sports goals in the sample appear to be large. A Chi-square test can be used to assess the extent to which these differences can be plausibly attributed to chance. The null and alternative hypotheses are H_0: there is no association between gender and sports goals, and H_a: there is an association between gender and sports goals.

To perform the χ^2 test of independence, follow these steps.

1. Click **Statistics**, click **Summarize**, and then click **Crosstabs**.
2. Click *goal*, then click ▶ to move *goal* into the "Row(s)" box.
3. Click *gender*, then click ▶ to move *gender* into the "Column(s)" box.
4. If you are interested in including the expected cell counts in the contingency table, click the **Cells** button and click **Expected** under **Counts** so that a check mark (✔) appears before **Expected**. If check marks appear before **Row**, **Column**, and **Total** under the "Percentages" box, click on each of these terms so that the check marks disappear. Then click **Continue**.
5. Click the **Statistics** button.
6. Click **Chi-Square**.
7. Click **Continue**.
8. Click **OK**.

The resulting SPSS output is shown in Tables 9.3 and 9.4.

**Example 9.1
(cont.)**

All of the expected cell counts are moderately large, so the χ^2 distribution should reasonably approximate the *P*-value. The test statistic value (Pearson Chi-square) is $\chi^{2*} = 24.898$ with $df = 3$ and a *P*-value (Asymptotic Significance) less than 0.001. The Chi-square test confirms that the data contain clear evidence against the null hypothesis that females and male students have the same distribution of sports goals. Under H_0, the chance of obtaining a value of χ^2 greater than or equal to the calculated value of 24.898 is very small – less than 0.001.

GOAL * GENDER Crosstabulation

			GENDER		
			Female	Male	Total
GOAL	HSC-HM	Count	14	31	45
		Expected Count	22.5	22.5	45.0
	HSC-LM	Count	7	18	25
		Expected Count	12.5	12.5	25.0
	LSC-HM	Count	21	5	26
		Expected Count	13.0	13.0	26.0
	LSC-LM	Count	25	13	38
		Expected Count	19.0	19.0	38.0
Total		Count	67	67	134
		Expected Count	67.0	67.0	134.0

Table 9.3

Chi-Square Tests

	Value	df	Asymp. Sig. (2-sided)
Pearson Chi-Square	24.898[a]	3	.000
Likelihood Ratio	26.036	3	.000
Linear-by-Linear Association	16.225	1	.000
N of Valid Cases	134		

a. 0 cells (.0%) have expected count less than 5. The minimum expected count is 12.50.

Table 9.4

Chapter 10. Inference for Regression

The descriptive analysis discussed in Chapter 2 for relations among two quantitative variables leads to formal inference. This chapter focuses on demonstrating how SPSS can be used to perform inference for **simple linear regression**.

Example 10.1 **(IPS Ex. 10.1)**	In practice, fat content is found by measuring body density, the weight per unit volume of the body. High fat content corresponds to low body density. Body density, denoted DEN, is hard to measure directly — the standard method requires that subjects be weighed underwater. For this reason, scientists have sought variables that are easier to measure and that can be used to predict body density. To measure skinfold thickness, a fold of skin is pinched between calipers at four predetermined locations and the four resulting measurements are added together. LSKIN is the natural logarithm of the sum of these four thicknesses. It is of interest to determine whether a linear relationship exists between DEN and LSKIN and to model any such relationship. A scatterplot of the variables DEN and LSKIN confirms that a linear relationship exists. Directions on how to construct a scatterplot appear in Section 2.1. It is now of interest to model this relationship.

To obtain the correlation and the least squares regression line, follow these steps.

1. Click **Statistics**, click **Regression**, and then click **Linear**. The SPSS window in Figure 2.3 appears with the variables *lskin* and *den*.
2. Click *lskin*, then click ▸ to move *lskin* into the "X Axis" box.
3. Click *den*, then click ▸ to move *den* into the "Y Axis" box.
4. If you are interested in a normal probability plot for the residuals, click the **Plots** box (Figure 10.1 appears). Select the **Normal probability plot** option in the "Standardized Residual Plots" box. Click **Continue**.

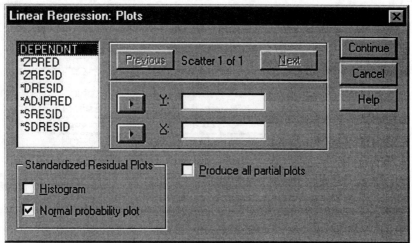

Figure 10.1

5. If you are interested in saving predicted values, residuals, distance measures, influential statistics, and prediction intervals, click the **Save** box (Figure 10.2 appears). Check the desired options and click **Continue**.
6. Click **OK**.

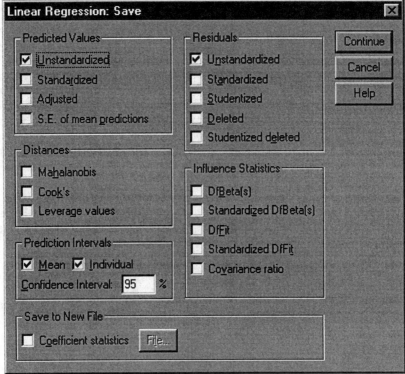

Figure 10.2

Tables 10.1 and 10.2 and Figure 10.3 are part of the resulting SPSS output.

Model Summary^b

Model	R	R Square	Adjusted R Square	Std. Error of the Estimate
1	.849^a	.720	.717	8.539E-03

a. Predictors: (Constant), LSKIN

b. Dependent Variable: DEN

Table 10.1

106

Coefficients[a]

Model		Unstandardized Coefficients		Standardized Coefficients	t	Sig.	95% Confidence Interval for B	
		B	Std. Error	Beta			Lower Bound	Upper Bound
1	(Constant)	1.163	.007		177.296	.000	1.150	1.176
	LSKIN	-6.31E-02	.004	-.849	-15.228	.000	-.071	-.055

a. Dependent Variable: DEN

Table 10.2

Normal P-P Plot of the Residuals

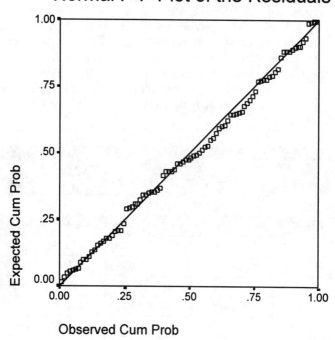

Figure 10.3

Example 10.1 (cont.)

Table 10.1 shows the correlation, the y intercept, and the slope. The correlation of $r = 0.849$ indicates that a strong, positive, linear association exists between DEN and LSKIN. In addition, the equation of the least squares regression line is

$$LSKIN = 1.163 - 0.0631DEN.$$

The estimated standard deviation of the model (often referred to as the MSE) is 0.008539.

Example 10.1 (cont.)

Now that a fitted model has been developed, the residuals of the model should be examined. Figure 10.3 is a normal probability plot of the standardized residuals. Since the plotted values are fairly linear, the assumption of normality seems reasonable. In addition, we can examine whether the residuals display any systematic pattern when plotted against other variables. Recall that the unstandardized residuals (and various other values) were saved into the Data Editor in step 5. Figure 10.4 displays the Data Editor containing the values that were saved, and the variable *res_1* contains the residuals. Figure 10.5 is a scatterplot of *res_1* and *lskin*. No unusual patterns or values are observed.

Higher body fat reduces body density and increases skinfold thickness, so we might expect a negative association. The hypotheses appropriate for testing this conjecture are H_0: $\beta_1 = 0$ and H_a: $\beta_1 < 0$. According to Table 10.2, the computed test statistic $t = -15.228$ and the P-value < 0.001. This indicates that there is sufficient evidence to conclude that a strong negative relationship exists between DEN and LSKIN. [Note that, in general, the P-value is computed assuming a two-tailed alternative, and the one-tailed P-value is half of the two-sided P-value.] Table 10.2 also shows that a 95% confidence interval for β_1 is $(-0.071, -0.055)$. This indicates that an increase of 1 in the logarithm of the skinfold thickness measure is associated with a decrease of body density between 0.055 and 0.071.

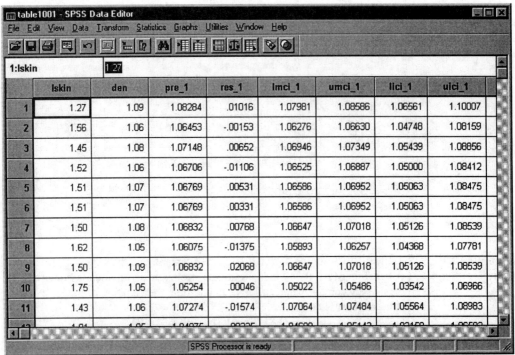

Figure 10.4

108

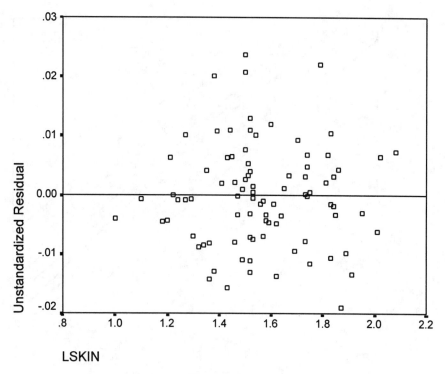

Figure 10.5

Example 10.1 (cont.)

It is also of interest to construct confidence intervals for the mean response and prediction intervals for a future observation. Figure 10.4 displays 95% confidence intervals for the mean response for each observation in the data set and 95% prediction intervals for future observations equal to each observation in the data set. The variables (*lmci_1*, *umci_1*) represent the 95% confidence interval, and the variables (*lici_1*, *uici_1*) represent the 95% prediction interval. In addition, the 95% confidence limits for the mean response (the inner bands) and the 95% prediction limits for the individual responses (the outer bands) for the body density example are displayed in Figure 10.6.

To generate a scatterplot with the regression equation, the confidence limits, and the prediction limits included, follow these steps.

1. Click **Graph**, click **Scatter**, and then click **Define**.
2. Click *lskin*, then click ⁍ to move *lskin* into the "X Axis" box.
3. Click *den*, then click ⁍ to move *den* into the "Y Axis" box.
4. Click **OK**.
5. Once in the Chart Editor, click **Chart**, click **Options**, and then click **Total**, which is found in the "Fit Line" box.

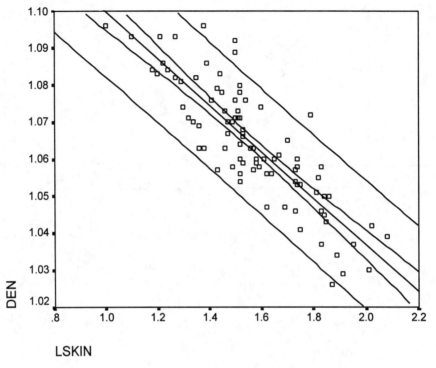

Figure 10.6

6. Click **Fit Options**. Figure 10.7 appears.
7. The Fit Method defaults to the desired "Linear regression" option. If confidence limits and prediction limits are desired, click on the desired options in the "Regression Prediction Line(s)" box. Then click **Continue**.
8. Click **OK**.

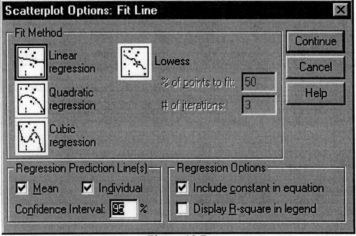

Figure 10.7

Chapter 11. Multiple Regression

This chapter focuses on using SPSS can be used to perform **multiple regression**. Multiple regression is a technique that is used when two or more explanatory variables are used to predict a dependent variable.

**Example 11.1
(IPS Ex. 11.1)**

The purpose of a study conducted at a large university was to attempt to predict the success of first-year computer science majors. One measure of success was the cumulative grade point average (GPA) after three semesters. Among the explanatory variables recorded at the time the students enrolled in the university were their SAT mathematics score (SATM), their SAT verbal score (SATV), and their average high school grades in mathematics (HSM), science (HSS), and English (HSE). Note that the high school grades are coded on a scale from 1 to 10, where A = 10, A– = 9, B+ = 8, and so on, but the GPA is coded on the traditional 4-point scale. There were 224 subjects in the study. An excerpt of the complete data set is given in Table 11.1. One objective is to examine the relationships between all the pairs of variables *gpa*, *satm*, *satv*, *hsm*, *hss*, and *hse* by computing all the pairwise correlations.

Table 11.1 GPA Data Set

Sub	GPA	SATM	SATV	HSM	HSS	HSE
001	3.32	670	600	10	10	10
002	2.26	700	640	6	8	5
.	.	.	.	.	.	.
.	.	.	.	.	.	.
.	.	.	.	.	.	.
223	2.59	630	470	5	4	7
224	2.28	559	488	9	8	9

To obtain all of the pairwise correlations, follow these steps.

1. Click **Statistics**, click **Correlate**, and then click **Bivariate**.
2. Click *gpa*, *hsm*, *hss*, *hse*, *satm*, and *satv* then click ▸ to move *gpa*, *hsm*, *hss*, *hse*, *satm*, and *satv* into the "Variables" box. This results in Figure 11.1.
3. Click **OK**.

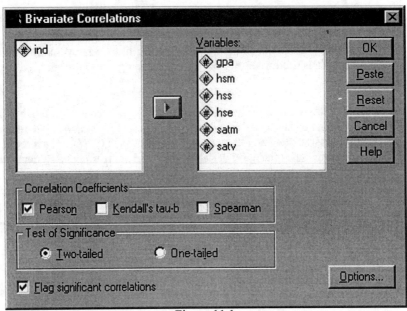

Figure 11.1

Table 11.2 is part of the resulting SPSS output.

Correlations

		GPA	HSM	HSS	HSE	SATM	SATV
GPA	Pearson Correlation	1.000	.436**	.329**	.289**	.252**	.114
	Sig. (2-tailed)	.	.000	.000	.000	.000	.087
	N	224	224	224	224	224	224
HSM	Pearson Correlation	.436**	1.000	.576**	.447**	.454**	.221**
	Sig. (2-tailed)	.000	.	.000	.000	.000	.001
	N	224	224	224	224	224	224
HSS	Pearson Correlation	.329**	.576**	1.000	.579**	.240**	.262**
	Sig. (2-tailed)	.000	.000	.	.000	.000	.000
	N	224	224	224	224	224	224
HSE	Pearson Correlation	.289**	.447**	.579**	1.000	.108	.244**
	Sig. (2-tailed)	.000	.000	.000	.	.106	.000
	N	224	224	224	224	224	224
SATM	Pearson Correlation	.252**	.454**	.240**	.108	1.000	.464**
	Sig. (2-tailed)	.000	.000	.000	.106	.	.000
	N	224	224	224	224	224	224
SATV	Pearson Correlation	.114	.221**	.262**	.244**	.464**	1.000
	Sig. (2-tailed)	.087	.001	.000	.000	.000	.
	N	224	224	224	224	224	224

**. Correlation is significant at the 0.01 level (2-tailed).

Table 11.2

112

Example 11.1
(cont.)

All the high school grades have higher correlations with GPA than SAT scores. For example, the correlation between GPA and HSM is 0.436. By examining the table of correlations, we can ascertain the strength of the relationships between the various pairwise variables.

Since all the high school grades have higher correlations with GPA than SAT scores, it is reasonable to model the response variable GPA using the explanatory variables HSM, HSS, and HSE.

To obtain the multiple regression equation, follow these steps.

1. Click **Statistics**, click **Regression**, and then click **Linear**.
2. Click *gpa*, then click ▸ to move *gpa* into the "Dependent" box.
3. Click *hsm*, *hss*, and *hse*, then click ▸ to move *hsm*, *hss*, and *hse* into the "Independent(s)" box. This results in Figure 11.2.
4. If you are interested in a normal probability plot for the residuals, click the **Plots** box. Select the **Normal probability plot** option in the "Standardized Residual Plots" box. Click **Continue**.
5. If you are interested in saving predicted values, residuals, distance measures, influential statistics, and prediction intervals, click the **Save** box. Check the desired options and click **Continue**.
6. Click **OK**.

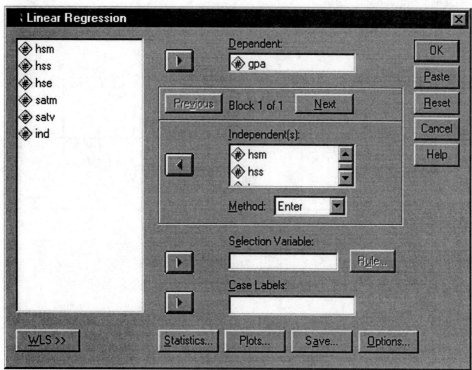

Figure 11.2

Tables 11.3 through 11.5 and Figure 11.3 are part of the resulting SPSS output.

Model Summary

Model	R	R Square	Adjusted R Square	Std. Error of the Estimate
1	.452[a]	.205	.194	.6998

a. Predictors: (Constant), HSE, HSM, HSS

Table 11.3

ANOVA[b]

Model		Sum of Squares	df	Mean Square	F	Sig.
1	Regression	27.712	3	9.237	18.861	.000[a]
	Residual	107.750	220	.490		
	Total	135.463	223			

a. Predictors: (Constant), HSE, HSM, HSS

b. Dependent Variable: GPA

Table 11.4

Coefficients[a]

Model		Unstandardized Coefficients		Standardized Coefficients	t	Sig.
		B	Std. Error	Beta		
1	(Constant)	.590	.294		2.005	.046
	HSM	.169	.035	.354	4.749	.000
	HSS	3.432E-02	.038	.075	.914	.362
	HSE	4.510E-02	.039	.087	1.166	.245

a. Dependent Variable: GPA

Table 11.5

Normal P-P Plot of the Residuals

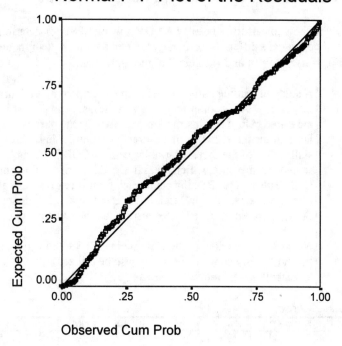

Figure 11.3

Example 11.1 (cont.)

Initially, we want to determine whether any of the variables are useful for predicting GPA. Specifically, the null and alternative hypotheses are H_0: $\beta_1 = \beta_2 = \beta_3 = 0$ and H_a: not all of the β_i are equal to 0. According to the ANOVA table in Table 11.4, the F statistic is 18.861 with a P-value < 0.001. Therefore, at least one of the regression coefficients differs from 0 in the fitted regression model

$$GPA = 0.590 + 0.169\,HSM + 0.0343\,HSS + 0.0451\,HSE.$$

Note that the coefficients for this model came from Table 11.5. In addition, the value for R^2 is 0.205, which is to say that approximately 20% of the variation in GPA is explained by high school grades in math, science, and English (found in Table 11.3).

The next step in the analysis is to determine which variables are useful in predicting GPA in the presence of the other variables. The variables and respective P-values from Table 11.5 are: HSM (P-value < 0.001), HSS (P-value $= 0.362$), and HSE (P-value $= 0.245$). Clearly, HSM is the most significant variable in the presence of the remaining two variables. Further analysis is necessary to determine the best model for predicting GPA.

Chapter 12. One-Way Analysis of Variance

This chapter describes how to perform **one-way ANOVA** using SPSS for determining whether the means from several populations differ. Specifically, the null and alternate hypotheses for one-way ANOVA are $H_0: \mu_1 = \mu_2 = \ldots = \mu_I$ and H_a: not all of the μ_i are equal.

**Example 12.1
(IPS Ex. 12.6)**

A study of reading comprehension in children compared three methods of instruction. As is common in such studies, several pretest variables were measured before any instruction was given. One purpose of the pretest was to see if the three groups of children were similar in their comprehension skills. One of the pretest variables called SCORE was an "intruded sentences" measure, which measures one type of reading comprehension skill. The data for 22 subjects in each group are given in Table 12.1. The three groups, which are Basal, DRTA, and Strategies (denoted in the table by Strat), represent the method of instruction the student subject will receive.

Note that when entering this data set into SPSS, the variable GROUP must be numerically coded (labels may also be utilized). In this example, codes and labels are as follows: 1 = Basal, 2 = DRTA, and 3 = Strat.

Table 12.1 Reading Scores

Sub	GROUP	SCORE	COMP	Sub	GROUP	SCORE	COMP	Sub	GROUP	SCORE	COMP
1	Basal	4	41	23	DRTA	7	31	45	Strat	11	53
2	Basal	6	41	24	DRTA	7	40	46	Strat	7	47
3	Basal	9	43	25	DRTA	12	48	47	Strat	4	41
4	Basal	12	46	26	DRTA	10	30	48	Strat	7	49
5	Basal	16	46	27	DRTA	16	42	49	Strat	7	43
6	Basal	15	45	28	DRTA	15	48	50	Strat	6	45
7	Basal	14	45	29	DRTA	9	49	51	Strat	11	50
8	Basal	12	32	30	DRTA	8	53	52	Strat	14	48
9	Basal	12	33	31	DRTA	13	48	53	Strat	13	49
10	Basal	8	39	32	DRTA	12	43	54	Strat	9	42
11	Basal	13	42	33	DRTA	7	55	55	Strat	12	38
12	Basal	9	45	34	DRTA	6	55	56	Strat	13	42
13	Basal	12	39	35	DRTA	8	57	57	Strat	4	34
14	Basal	12	44	36	DRTA	9	53	58	Strat	13	48
15	Basal	12	36	37	DRTA	9	37	59	Strat	6	51
16	Basal	10	49	38	DRTA	8	50	60	Strat	12	33
17	Basal	8	40	39	DRTA	9	54	61	Strat	6	44
18	Basal	12	35	40	DRTA	13	41	62	Strat	11	48
19	Basal	11	36	41	DRTA	10	49	63	Strat	14	49
20	Basal	8	40	42	DRTA	8	47	64	Strat	8	33
21	Basal	7	54	43	DRTA	8	49	65	Strat	5	45
22	Basal	9	32	44	DRTA	10	49	66	Strat	8	42

Example 12.1 (cont.)

Before proceeding with ANOVA, we must verify that the assumptions of (1) normally distributed data and (2) equality of standard deviations in the various groups are reasonably satisfied. Because the data appear reasonably normal (which can be demonstrated using normal quantile plots for the three groups of data) and the assumption of equal standard deviations is reasonably satisfied, we can proceed with ANOVA.

Initially, we want to analyze the pretest scores and determine whether the three groups had similar population means on this measure. Specifically, the null and alternative hypotheses are H_0: $\mu_B = \mu_D = \mu_S$ and H_a: not all of the μ_i are equal.

To perform one-way ANOVA, follow these steps.

1. Click **Statistics**, click **Compare Means**, and then click **One-Way ANOVA**. The SPSS window in Figure 12.1 appears.

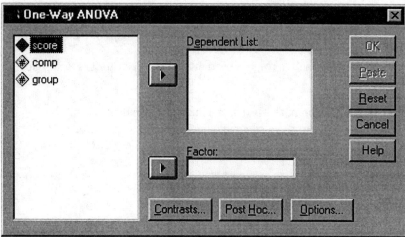

Figure 12.1

2. Click *score*, then click ▸ to move *score* into the "Dependent List" box.
3. Click *group*, then click ▸ to move *group* into the "Factor" box.
4. Click **OK**.

Table 12.2 is the resulting SPSS output.

ANOVA

SCORE

	Sum of Squares	df	Mean Square	F	Sig.
Between Groups	20.576	2	10.288	1.132	.329
Within Groups	572.455	63	9.087		
Total	593.030	65			

Table 12.2

Example 12.1 (cont.)

A *P*-value of 0.329 implies that there is no reason to reject H_0 that the three groups have equal population means on this measure. This was the desired outcome. We now turn to the response variable, a measure of reading comprehension called *comp*, that was measured by a test taken after the instruction was completed. Initially, we are interested in comparing several summary statistics for *comp* in the three groups of the study.

To obtain descriptive statistics for a response variable for each category of the grouping variable, follow these steps.

1. Click **Statistics**, click **Compare Means**, and then click **Means**.
2. Click *comp*, then click ▸ to move *comp* into the "Dependent List" box.
3. Click *group*, then click ▸ to move *group* into the "Independent List" box. The SPSS window in Figure 12.2 appears.
4. If you are interested in choosing summary statistics options, click the **Options** box. Choose the desired summary statistics, and click **Continue.**
5. Click **OK**.

Figure 12.2

Table 12.3 is the resulting SPSS output.

Report

COMP

GROUP	Mean	N	Std. Deviation
Basal	41.045	22	5.636
DRTA	46.727	22	7.388
Strat	44.273	22	5.767
Total	44.015	66	6.644

Table 12.3

Example 12.1 (cont.)

Given the preceding results, we are interested in analyzing the *comp* scores to determine whether the three groups have similar population means for this measure. Specifically, the hypotheses of interest are H_0: $\mu_B = \mu_D = \mu_S$ and H_a: not all of the μ_i are equal. In addition, the instruction for the Basal group was the standard method commonly used in the schools, and the DRTA and Strat groups received innovative methods of teaching that are designed to improve reading comprehension. The researcher is interested in two primary questions: (1) whether the two new methods are better than the standard method and (2) whether the two new methods differ. These questions can be formulated using the following hypotheses:

$$H_{01}: 0.5(\mu_D + \mu_S) = \mu_B \quad \text{versus} \quad H_{a1}: 0.5(\mu_D + \mu_S) > \mu_B$$

and

$$H_{02}: \mu_D = \mu_S \quad \text{versus} \quad H_{a2}: \mu_D \neq \mu_S.$$

These null hypotheses can be formulated using the two contrasts:

$$\psi_1 = (-1)\mu_B + (0.5)\mu_D + (0.5)\mu_S$$

and

$$\psi_2 = (0)\mu_B + (1)\mu_D + (-1)\mu_S.$$

To perform a one-way ANOVA with planned contrasts, follow these steps.

1. Click **Statistics**, click **Compare Means**, and then click **One-Way ANOVA**.
2. Click *comp*, then click ‣ to move *comp* into the "Dependent List" box.
3. Click *group*, then click ‣ to move *group* into the "Factor" box.
4. If you are interested in using contrasts, click the **Contrasts** box. Enter the coefficients of your first contrast. After each coefficient, click **Add**. After each contrast is complete, click **Next**. The SPSS window in Figure 12.3 appears. After the last contrast is entered, click **Continue**.

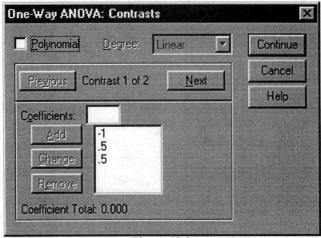

Figure 12.3

5. Click **OK**.

Tables 12.4 through 12.6 are the resulting SPSS output.

ANOVA

COMP

	Sum of Squares	df	Mean Square	F	Sig.
Between Groups	357.303	2	178.652	4.481	.015
Within Groups	2511.682	63	39.868		
Total	2868.985	65			

Table 12.4

Contrast Coefficients

	GROUP		
Contrast	Basal	DRTA	Strat
1	-1	.5	.5
2	0	1	-1

Table 12.5

Contrast Tests

		Contrast	Value of Contrast	Std. Error	t	df	Sig. (2-tailed)
COMP	Assume equal variances	1	4.455	1.649	2.702	63	.009
		2	2.455	1.904	1.289	63	.202
	Does not assume equal variances	1	4.455	1.563	2.851	47.945	.006
		2	2.455	1.998	1.228	39.661	.227

Table 12.6

Example 12.1 (cont.)

Since the P-value is 0.015 (from Table 12.4), there is sufficient evidence to reject H_0 in favor of H_a. This indicates that some μ_i differs. In addition, since the P-value in Table 12.6 for the first contrast is 0.0045 (0.009/2), there is sufficient evidence to reject H_{01} in favor of H_{a1}. This indicates that new methods produce higher scores than the old. Since the P-value for the second contrast is 0.202, there is insufficient evidence to reject H_{02} that the means for the two new methods are equal.

In many studies specific questions cannot be formulated in advance. As before, the hypotheses of interest are H_0: $\mu_B = \mu_D = \mu_S$ and H_a: not all of the μ_i are equal. In addition, if H_0 is rejected, we would like to know which means differ. Two procedures that are commonly used for multiple comparisons are the least-significant differences (LSD) method and the Bonferroni method.

To perform a one-way ANOVA with post hoc multiple comparisons, follow these steps.

1. Click **Statistics**, click **Compare Means**, and then click **One-Way ANOVA**.
2. Click *comp*, then click ▸ to move *comp* into the "Dependent List" box.
3. Click *group*, then click ▸ to move *group* into the "Factor" box.
4. If you are interested in multiple comparisons, you can click on the **Post Hoc** box. The SPSS window in Figure 12.4 appears. Click on the desired multiple comparison test procedure, and click **Continue**.

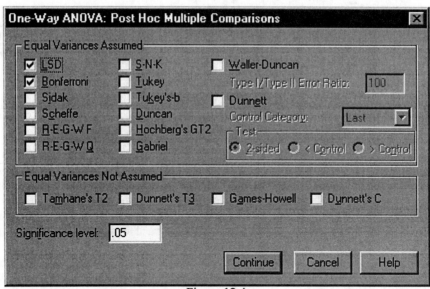

Figure 12.4

5. If you are interested in descriptive statistics or a means plot, you can click on the **Options** box, click on the desired options, and click **Continue.**
6. Click **OK**.

For illustration purposes, SPSS output from a means plot (Figure 12.5) and both the LSD and the Bonferroni methods (Table 12.7) have been provided.

Example 12.1 (cont.) | The ANOVA table (which is the same as Table 12.4) indicates that some μ_i differs. The output of the multiple comparisons tables indicates significantly different means with an asterisk (*). Both the LSD and the Bonferroni methods indicate that the means for the Basal and the DRTA groups differ.

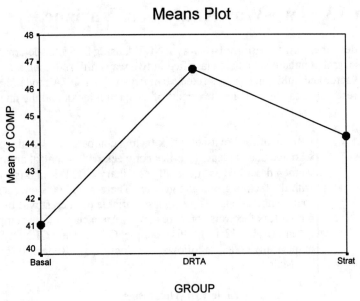

Means Plot

Figure 12.5

Multiple Comparisons

Dependent Variable: COMP

	(I) GROUP	(J) GROUP	Mean Difference (I-J)	Std. Error	Sig.	95% Confidence Interval Lower Bound	95% Confidence Interval Upper Bound
LSD	Basal	DRTA	-5.682*	1.904	.004	-9.486	-1.877
		Strat	-3.227	1.904	.095	-7.032	.577
	DRTA	Basal	5.682*	1.904	.004	1.877	9.486
		Strat	2.455	1.904	.202	-1.350	6.259
	Strat	Basal	3.227	1.904	.095	-.577	7.032
		DRTA	-2.455	1.904	.202	-6.259	1.350
Bonferroni	Basal	DRTA	-5.682*	1.904	.012	-10.364	-.999
		Strat	-3.227	1.904	.285	-7.910	1.455
	DRTA	Basal	5.682*	1.904	.012	.999	10.364
		Strat	2.455	1.904	.606	-2.228	7.137
	Strat	Basal	3.227	1.904	.285	-1.455	7.910
		DRTA	-2.455	1.904	.606	-7.137	2.228

*. The mean difference is significant at the .05 level.

Table 12.7

Chapter 13. Two-Way Analysis of Variance

This chapter describes how to perform **two-way ANOVA** using SPSS for determining whether the means from several populations that are classified in two ways differ. Recall that one-way designs vary a single factor and hold other factors fixed. In a two-way ANOVA model there are two factors. The researcher can investigate the effects of each main factor and the interaction between the factors.

Example 13.1
(IPS Ex. 13.8)

A study of cardiovascular risk factors compared men and women runners who averaged at least 15 miles per week with a control group of men and women described as "generally sedentary." The design is a 2×2 ANOVA with the factors group and gender. There were 200 subjects in each of the four combinations. The response variable of interest was the heart rate after 6 minutes of exercise on a treadmill. An excerpt of the complete dataset is given in Table 13.1. In this example, GROUP and GENDER must be numerically coded as follows: 0 = Control, 1 = Runner, 0 = Female, and 1 = Male.

Table 13.1 Heart Rate

Sub	GROUP	GENDER	RATE
001	Control	Female	159
002	Control	Female	183
003	Control	Female	140
.	.	.	.
.	.	.	.
.	.	.	.
798	Runner	Male	112
799	Runner	Male	97
800	Runner	Male	89

Before proceeding with ANOVA, we must verify that the assumptions of (1) normally distributed data and (2) equality of standard deviations in the various groups are reasonably satisfied. Because the data appear reasonably normal (which can be demonstrated using normal quantile plots for the four groups of data) and the assumption of equal standard deviations is reasonably satisfied, we can proceed with ANOVA.

Initially, we are interested in comparing several summary statistics for each of the four combinations of the factors of the study. Table 13.2 is the result of SPSS analysis (the instructions will be given later in this chapter).

Inspection of Table 13.2 indicates that there may be a difference in the means between the groups and the genders. Therefore, we are interested in analyzing data to determine whether the factors influence the mean heart rate.

Descriptive Statistics

Dependent Variable: RATE

GROUP	GENDER	Mean	Std. Deviation	N
Control	Female	148.0000	16.2709	200
	Male	130.0000	17.1004	200
	Total	139.0000	18.9496	400
Runner	Female	115.9850	15.9715	200
	Male	103.9750	12.4994	200
	Total	109.9800	15.5338	400
Total	Female	131.9925	22.7189	400
	Male	116.9875	19.8372	400
	Total	124.4900	22.5969	800

Table 13.2

To perform this two-way ANOVA, follow these steps.

1. Click **Statistics**, click **General Linear Model**, and then click **GLM-General Factorial**. The SPSS window in Figure 13.1 appears.

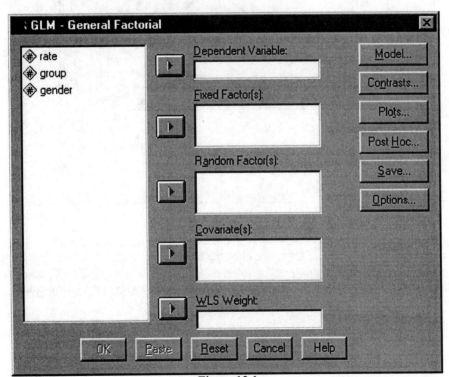

Figure 13.1

2. Click *rate*, then click ▸ to move *rate* into the "Dependent Variable" box.
3. Click *group* and *gender*, then click ▸ to move *group* and *gender* into the "Fixed Factor(s)" box.
4. The default model for SPSS is the full factorial model (i.e., the model that has all the main effects and interaction effects) computed using type III sums of squares. If you are interested in specifying a custom model, click the **Model** box. Click the **Custom** circle and choose the desired terms for the model (main effects, interaction terms, etc.). In addition, you can choose the desired sum of squares for the model (type I, II, III, or IV), and click **Continue**. In our example, we selected the type I sums of squares.
5. If you are interested in using contrasts, click the **Contrasts** box. Choose the desired type of contrast. After the selection of the contrasts are complete, click **Continue**.
6. If you are interested in constructing a means plot, click the **Plots** box. The SPSS window in Figure 13.2 appears. Click *group*, then click ▸ to move *group* into the "Horizontal Axis" box. Click *gender*, then click ▸ to move *gender* into the "Separate Lines" box. Click **Add**, and then click **Continue**.

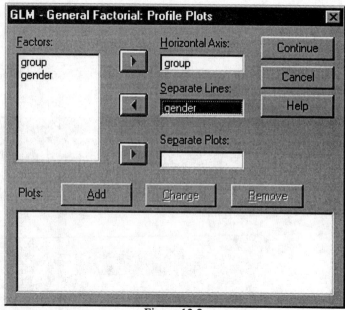

Figure 13.2

7. If you are interested in comparing several summary statistics for each of the four combinations of the factors of the study, click the **Options** box. The SPSS window in Figure 13.3 appears. Click *group* and *gender*, then click ▸ to move *group* and *gender* into the "Display Means" box. Click the **Descriptive Statistics** box, and then click **Continue**.
8. Click **OK**.

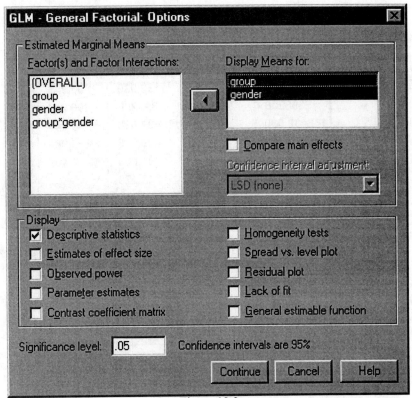
Figure 13.3

Tables 13.3 and 13.4 and Figure 13.4 are the resulting SPSS output. In addition, step 7 yields the table of descriptive statistics that was displayed in Table 13.2.

Between-Subjects Factors

		Value Label	N
GROUP	0	Control	400
	1	Runner	400
GENDER	0	Female	400
	1	Male	400

Table 13.3

Tests of Between-Subjects Effects

Dependent Variable: RATE

Source	Type I Sum of Squares	df	Mean Square	F	Sig.
Corrected Model	215256.090[a]	3	71752.030	296.345	.000
Intercept	12398208	1	12398208	51206.259	.000
GROUP	168432.080	1	168432.080	695.647	.000
GENDER	45030.005	1	45030.005	185.980	.000
GROUP * GENDER	1794.005	1	1794.005	7.409	.007
Error	192729.830	796	242.123		
Total	12806194	800			
Corrected Total	407985.920	799			

a. R Squared = .528 (Adjusted R Squared = .526)

Table 13.4

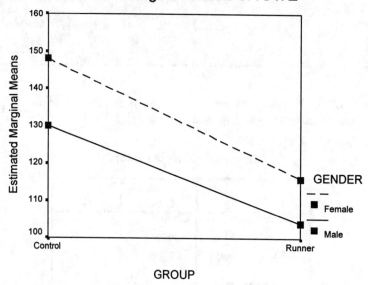

Figure 13.4

128

Example 13.1 (cont.)

All three effects (*group*, *gender*, and the interaction of *group*gender*) are statistically significant (see Table 13.4). To interpret these results, we can examine the plot of means on Figure 13.4. The significance of the main effect for *group* is demonstrated by the fact that the mean heart rate for the control group exceeds the mean heart rate for the runner group for both genders. The significance of the main effect of *gender* is demonstrated by the fact that the mean heart rate for females exceeds that of males for each group. The significance of the interaction of *group*gender* is demonstrated by the fact that the two lines are not parallel. This indicates that the difference in the mean heart rate between the control and runner groups is greater for women ($148 - 116 = 32$) than for men ($130 - 104 = 26$). As Figure 13.4 suggests, the interaction effect is not large, but (due to the sample size) it is statistically significant.

Chapter 14. Nonparametric Tests

This chapter introduces one type of **nonparametric** procedures, tests that can replace *t* tests and one-way analysis of variance when the normality assumption for those tests is not met. When distributions are strongly skewed, the mean may not be the preferred measure of center. The focus of these tests is on medians rather than means. All three of these tests utilize ranks of the observations in calculating the test statistic.

Section 14.1. Wilcoxon Rank Sum Test

The **Wilcoxon rank sum test** is the nonparametric counterpart of the parametric independent *t* test. It is applied to situations in which the normality assumption underlying the parametric independent *t* test has been violated or questionably met. The focus of this test is on medians rather than means.   An alternate form of this test, the one used by SPSS, is the Mann-Whitney *U* test.

**Example 14.1
(IPS Ex. 14.6)**

Food sold at outdoor fairs and festivals may be less safe than food sold in restaurants because it is prepared in temporary locations and often by volunteer help. What do people who attend fairs think about the safety of food served? One study asked this question of people at a number of fairs in the Midwest:

How often do you think people become sick because of food they consume prepared at outdoor fairs and festivals? The possible responses were: 1 = very rarely, 2 = once in a while, 3 = often, 4 = more often than not, and 5 = always.

In all, 303 people answered the question. Of these, 196 were women and 107 were men. Is there good evidence that men and women differ in their perceptions about food safety at fairs? The data are presented in Table 14.1 as a two-way table of counts.

Table 14.1 Responses by Gender

Gender	Responses					Total
	1	2	3	4	5	
Female	13	108	50	23	2	196
Male	22	57	22	5	1	107
Total	35	165	72	28	3	303

We would like to know whether men or women are more concerned about food safety. Whereas a Chi-square test could be applied to answer the general question, this test ignores the ordering of the responses and so does not use all of the available information. Since the data are ordinal, a test based on ranks makes sense. One can use the Wilcoxon rank sum test for the hypotheses

Example 14.1
(cont.)

H_0: men and women do not differ in their responses
H_a: one of the two genders gives systematically larger
responses than the other.

The data were entered into SPSS using ten rows and three columns with the variable names *gender* (declared numeric 8.0 with value labels 1 = Female and 2 = Male), *sick* (declared numeric 8.0 with value labels 1 = very rarely, 2 = once in a while, 3 = often, 4 = more often than not, and 5 = always), and *weight* (declared numeric 8.0) where *weight* represents the count of individuals for each gender who selected each of the five response options. It is important to note that the grouping variable (in this case *gender*) must be a numeric variable (not entered as M's and F's). Also, prior to performing any analyses, the weighting option under **Data** and **Weight Cases** was activated (see Example 2.2 in Chapter 2 for an example of how to enter these data and how to activate the weighting option).

To conduct a Wilcoxon rank sum test (or Mann-Whitney *U* test), follow these steps.

1. Click **Statistics**, click **Nonparametric Tests**, and then click **2 Independent Samples**. The "Two-Independent Samples Tests" window in Figure 14.1 appears.

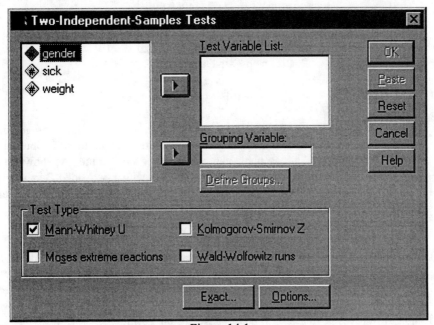

Figure 14.1

2. Click *sick*, then click ▸ to move *sick* into the "Test Variable List" box.
3. Click *gender*, then click ▸ to move *gender* into the "Grouping Variable" box.
4. Click the **Define Groups** button.
5. Type **1** in the "Group 1" box , press the **Tab** key, and type **2** in the "Group 2" box.
6. Click **Continue**.

7. The default test is the Mann-Whitney U test (as indicated by the ✔ in front of Mann-Whitney U in the "Test Type" area).
8. Click **OK**.

The resulting output is displayed in Tables 14.2 and 14.3.

Ranks

	GENDER	N	Mean Rank	Sum of Ranks
SICK	Female	196	163.25	31996.50
	Male	107	131.40	14059.50
	Total	303		

Table 14.2

Test Statistics[a]

	SICK
Mann-Whitney U	8281.500
Wilcoxon W	14059.500
Z	-3.334
Asymp. Sig. (2-tailed)	.001

a. Grouping Variable: GENDER

Table 14.3

Example 14.1 (cont.)

As can be seen in Table 14.2, the rank sum for men (using average ranks for ties) is $W = 14,059.5$. Since the sample size is large, the z distribution should yield a reasonable approximation of the P-value. As shown in Table 14.3, the standardized value is $z = -3.334$ with a two-sided P-value $= 0.001$. This small P-value lends strong evidence that women are more concerned than men about the safety of food served at fairs.

Note: The output shown in Tables 14.2 and 14.3 was generated using the data in Table 14.1 (from Example 14.6 in IPS). There is a slight disagreement between the values contained in the output from IPS and the values contained in Tables 14.2 and 14.3 of this manual. The output in IPS was generated using the data set on the CD-ROM and there is a data entry error in this file. This produces slight differences in values for S and z as well as the P-value.

Section 14.2. Wilcoxon Signed Rank Test

This section will introduce the **Wilcoxon signed rank test**, the nonparametric counterpart of a paired-samples *t* test. It is used in situations in which there are repeated measures (the same group is assessed on the same measure on two occasions) or matched subjects (pairs of individuals are each assessed once on a measure). It is applied to situations in which the assumptions underlying the parametric *t* test have been violated or questionably met. The focus of this test is on medians rather than means.

Example 14.2 (IPS Ex. 14.11)	The golf scores of 12 members of a college women's golf team in two rounds of tournament play are shown in Table 14.4. A golf score is the number of strokes required to complete the course; therefore, low scores are better.

Table 14.4

Player	1	2	3	4	5	6	7	8	9	10	11	12
Round 2	94	85	89	89	81	76	107	89	87	91	88	80
Round 1	89	90	87	95	86	81	102	105	83	88	91	79
Difference	5	-5	2	-6	-5	-5	5	-16	4	3	-3	1

The data were entered into SPSS using two columns and the variable names **round_1** (declared numeric 8.0) and **round_2** (declared numeric 8.0). The variables **round_1** and **round_2** were entered into the first and second columns, respectively.

Because this is a matched pairs design, inference is based on the differences between pairs. Negative differences indicate better (lower) scores on the second round. We see that 6 of the 12 golfers improved their scores. We would like to test the hypotheses that in a large population of collegiate women golfers

H_0: scores have the same distribution in Rounds 1 and 2
H_a: scores are systematically lower or higher in Round 2.

The assessment of whether the assumption of normality has been met is based on the difference in golf scores (see Section 7.3 on the matched pairs *t* test for instructions in generating the difference variable). A small sample makes it difficult to assess normality adequately, but the normal quantile plot of the differences in Figure 14.2 shows some irregularity and a low outlier. As such, one should use the Wilcoxon signed rank test, which does not require normality.

Normal P-P Plot of DIFF

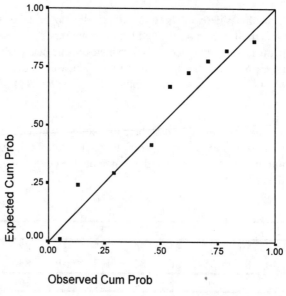

Figure 14.2

To conduct a Wilcoxon signed rank test, follow these steps.

1. Click **Statistics**, click **Nonparametric Tests**, and then click **2 Related Samples**. The "Two-Related Samples Tests" window shown in Figure 14.3 appears.
2. Click *round_1* and it appears after "Variable 1" in the "Current Selections" box.

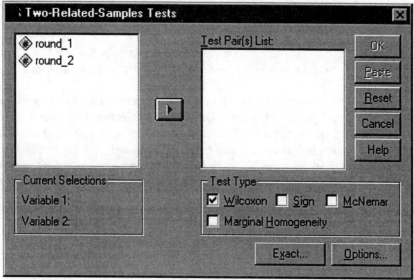

Figure 14.3

3. Click *round_2* and it appears after "Variable 2" in the "Current Selections" box.
4. Click ‣ to move the variables into the "Test Pair(s) List" box (it will read "*round_1 – round_2*").
5. The default test is the Wilcoxon signed rank test (as indicated by the ✔ in front of Wilcoxon in the "Test Type" box).
6. Click **OK**.

The resulting SPSS output is displayed in Tables 14.5 and 14.6.

Ranks

		N	Mean Rank	Sum of Ranks
ROUND_2 - ROUND_1	Negative Ranks	6ᵃ	8.42	50.50
	Positive Ranks	6ᵇ	4.58	27.50
	Ties	0ᶜ		
	Total	12		

a. ROUND_2 < ROUND_1

b. ROUND_2 > ROUND_1

c. ROUND_1 = ROUND_2

Table 14.5

Test Statisticsᵇ

	ROUND_2 - ROUND_1
Z	-.910ᵃ
Asymp. Sig. (2-tailed)	.363

a. Based on positive ranks.

b. Wilcoxon Signed Ranks Test

Table 14.6

Example 14.2 (cont.)

First, notice that the difference in Table 14.5 reads "ROUND_2 – ROUND_1", which is the reverse of the difference variable that appeared to be created in Step 4 (*round_1 – round_2*). For this test, SPSS always creates a difference score between the two named variables based on the order in which the variables are entered in the data set. The variable that appears <u>first</u> in the data set is always subtracted from the variable that appears <u>later</u> in the data set. For this problem, the variables were entered in the order of *round_1* and then *round_2*. Thus, SPSS creates a difference score of *round_2* minus *round_1*, despite the order in which the variables appear in the "Test(s) Pairs List" box in the "Two-Related Samples Tests"

Example 14.2 (cont.)	window. The same conclusion will be reached regardless of the order in which subtraction was done as the two-tailed *P*-value will be the same whether the difference is ***round_2 – round_1*** or ***round_1 – round_2***. However, caution must be used in performing a directional test.
	As shown in Table 14.5, the sum of the Negative Ranks (ROUND_2 < ROUND_1) is 50.5 and the sum of the Positive Ranks (ROUND_2 > ROUND_1) is 27.5. The value of 0 for Ties means that there were no pairs of scores in which the values were the same (e.g., ROUND_2 = ROUND_1 (it does not mean that there were no ties among the ranks)). The Wilcoxon signed rank statistic is the sum of the positive differences. The value is W^+ = 27.5. In Table 14.6, a *z* value of -0.91 is reported that is based on the standardized sum of the positive ranks and is not adjusted for the continuity correction. The corresponding *P*-value is given as 0.363. These data give no evidence for a systematic change in scores between rounds.

Section 14.3. Kruskal-Wallis Test

The **Kruskal-Wallis test** is the nonparametric counterpart of the parametric one-way analysis of variance. It is applied to situations in which the normality assumption underlying the parametric one-way ANOVA has been violated or questionably met. The focus of this test is on medians rather than means.

Example 14.3 (IPS Ex. 14.13)	Lamb's-quarter is a common weed that interferes with the growth of corn. A researcher planted corn at the same rate in 16 small plots of ground, then randomly assigned plots to four groups. He weeded the plots by hand to allow a fixed number of Lamb's-quarters to grow in each meter of a corn row. These numbers were 0, 1, 3, and 9 in the four groups of plots. No other weeds were allowed to grow, and all plots received identical treatment except for the weeds. The yields of corn (bushels per acre) in each of the plots are shown in Table 14.7. The summary statistics for the data are shown in Table 14.8.

Table 14.7 Yields of Corn

Weeds per meter	Yield (bushels/acre)			
0	166.7	172.2	165.0	176.9
1	166.2	157.3	166.7	161.1
3	158.6	176.4	153.1	156.0
9	162.8	142.4	162.7	162.4

Table 14.8 Descriptive Statistics for Yield

Weeds per meter	n	Mean	Std. Dev.
0	4	170.200	5.422
1	4	162.825	4.469
3	4	161.025	10.493
9	4	157.575	10.118

Example 14.3 (cont.)

The sample standard deviations do not satisfy the rule of thumb from IPS for use of ANOVA, that the largest standard deviation should not exceed twice the smallest. Normal quantile plots show that outliers are present in the yields for 3 and 9 weeds per meter. These are the correct yields for their plots, so we have no justification for removing them. We may want to use a nonparametric test.

The null hypothesis H_0: yields have the same distribution in all groups is being tested against the one-sided alternative H_a: yields are systematically higher in some groups than in others.

The data were entered in two columns using the variables of *weeds* (declared numeric 8.0) and *yield* (declared numeric 8.1). It is important to note that the grouping variable (in this case *weeds*) must always be a numeric variable. To conduct a Kruskal-Wallis *H* test, follow these steps.

1. Click **Statistics**, click **Nonparametrics Tests**, and then click **K Independent Samples**. The SPSS window shown in Figure 14.4 will appear.

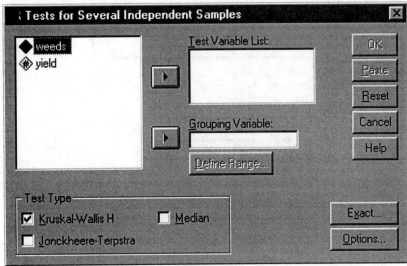

Figure 14.4

2. Click *yield*, then click ▶ to move *yield* into the "Test Variable List" box.
3. Click *weed*, then click ▶ to move *weed* into the "Grouping Variable" box.
4. Click **Define Range**.
5. Type **0** in the "Minimum" box, press the **Tab** key, and type **9** in the "Maximum" box.
6. Click **Continue**.
7. The default test is the Kruskal-Wallis H Test (as indicated by the ✔ in front of Kruskal-Wallis H in the "Test Type" box).
8. Click **OK**.

Example 14.3 (cont.)

Examination of Table 14.8 suggests that an increase in weeds results in decreased yield. The output from the analysis is shown in Tables 14.9 and 14.10. As can be seen in Table 14.9, the mean rank for the group with 0 weeds per meter was 13.13, the mean rank for the group with 1 weed per meter was 8.38, the mean rank for the group with 3 weeds per meter was 6.25, and the mean rank for the group with 9 weeds per meter was 6.25. SPSS uses the Chi-square approximation to obtain a P-value = 0.134, as shown in Table 14.10. This small experiment suggests that more weeds decrease yield but does not provide convincing evidence that weeds have an effect.

Ranks

	WEEDS	N	Mean Rank
YIELD	0	4	13.13
	1	4	8.38
	3	4	6.25
	9	4	6.25
	Total	16	

Table 14.9

Test Statistics[a,b]

	YIELD
Chi-Square	5.573
df	3
Asymp. Sig.	.134

a. Kruskal Wallis Test

b. Grouping Variable: WEEDS

Table 14.10

Chapter 15. Logistic Regression

Logistic regression models are used to model the relationship between a response variable that has only two values (success and failure) and one or more explanatory variables. Specifically, logistic regression models the natural logarithm of the odds of success using the model

$$\log\left(\frac{p}{1-p}\right) = \beta_0 + \beta_1 x$$

where p is the proportion of success and x is the explanatory variable. This chapter describes how to perform **logistic regression** using SPSS.

Example 15.1
(IPS Ex. 15.7)

An experiment was designed to examine how well the insecticide rotenone kills aphids that feed on chrysanthemum plants. The explanatory variable is the log concentration (in milligrams per liter) of the insecticide. At each concentration, approximately 50 insects were exposed. Each insect was either killed or not killed. The results are given in Table 15.1.

Table 15.1

Concentration (log)	Num. of Insects	Num. Killed
0.96	50	6
1.33	48	16
1.63	46	24
2.04	49	42
2.32	50	44

Logistic regression can be used to model the relationship between the response variable, log odds of the proportion killed, and the explanatory variable, concentration. In order to enter the data for this problem into SPSS the data set should be coded as displayed in Table 15.2. Note that when entering the data, the variable *killed* should be weighted using the variable *freq*. (See Section 2.3 for directions on the weight option.)

Table 15.2

Killed	Concentration (log)	Frequency
0	0.96	44
1	0.96	6
0	1.33	32
1	1.33	16
0	1.63	22
1	1.63	24
0	2.04	7
1	2.04	42
0	2.32	6
1	2.32	44

To perform this logistic regression, follow these steps.

1. Click **Statistics**, click **Regression**, and then click **Logistic**. The SPSS window in Figure 15.1 appears.

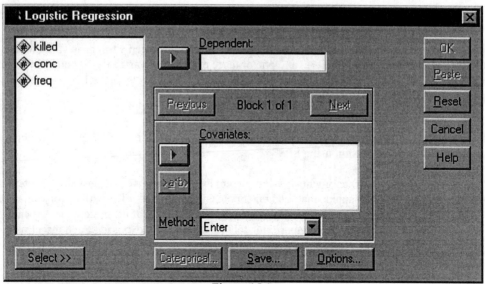

Figure 15.1

2. Click *killed*, then click ▸ to move *killed* into the "Dependent Variable" box.
3. Click *conc*, then click ▸ to move *conc* into the "Covariates" box.
4. If you are interested in a confidence interval for the odds ratio, click the **Options** box. Click the **CI for exp(B)** option, and then click **Continue.**
5. Click **OK**.

Table 15.3 is part of the resulting SPSS output.

```
Dependent Variable..   KILLED

Variable(s) Entered on Step Number
1..        CONC

                      Chi-Square    df Significance

   Model                 95.234      1       .0000
   Block                 95.234      1       .0000

----------------- Variables in the Equation ------------------

Variable          B        S.E.      Wald      df      Sig        R

CONC          3.1088      .3879   64.2332       1    .0000     .4310
Constant     -4.8923      .6426   57.9606       1    .0000


                       95% CI for Exp(B)
Variable      Exp(B)     Lower      Upper

CONC         22.3936    10.4701    47.8958
```

Table 15.3

Example 15.1 (cont.)

From the SPSS output one observes that the fitted model is

$$\log\left(\frac{p}{1-p}\right) = \log(odds) = -4.89 + 3.11x$$

where x is the log concentration. In addition, there is sufficient evidence to reject the null hypothesis that $\beta_1 = 0$ in favor of the alternative hypothesis that $\beta_1 \neq 0$ (since $\chi^2 = 64.23$ and P-value < 0.0001). The odds ratio, given by Exp(B), is 22.39. This indicates that an increase in 1 unit in the log concentration of the insecticide results in a 22-fold increase in the odds that an insect will be killed. The 95% confidence interval for the odds ratio is (10.47, 47.90).

Example 15.2 (IPS Ex. 15.5)

A study is conducted to examine TASTE, a measure of the quality of a particular kind of cheese. In this example, the cheese is classified as acceptable (TASTEOK=1) if TASTE is greater than or equal to 37 and unacceptable (TASTEOK=0) if TASTE is less than 37. The data set contains three explanatory variables, ACETIC, H2S, and LACTIC, which are the transformed concentrations of acetic acid, hydrogen sulfide, and lactic acid, respectively. Table 15.4 displays the data set (to preserve space TASTEOK is denoted by OK, ACETIC is denoted by ACE, and LACTIC is denoted by LAC).

Table 15.4

Sub	TASTE	OK	ACE	H2S	LAC	Sub	TASTE	OK	ACE	H2S	LAC
1	12.3	0	4.543	3.135	0.86	16	40.9	1	6.365	9.588	1.74
2	20.9	0	5.159	5.043	1.53	17	15.9	0	4.787	3.912	1.16
3	39.0	1	5.366	5.438	1.57	18	6.4	0	5.412	4.700	1.49
4	47.9	1	5.759	7.496	1.81	19	18.0	0	5.247	6.174	1.63
5	5.6	0	4.663	3.807	0.99	20	38.9	1	5.438	9.064	1.99
6	25.9	0	5.697	7.601	1.09	21	14.0	0	4.564	4.949	1.15
7	37.3	1	5.892	8.726	1.29	22	15.2	0	5.298	5.220	1.33
8	21.9	0	6.078	7.966	1.78	23	32.0	0	5.455	9.242	1.44
9	18.1	0	4.898	3.850	1.29	24	56.7	1	5.855	10.199	2.01
10	21.0	0	5.242	4.174	1.58	25	16.8	0	5.366	3.664	1.31
11	34.9	0	5.740	6.142	1.68	26	11.6	0	6.043	3.219	1.46
12	57.2	1	6.446	7.908	1.90	27	26.5	0	6.458	6.962	1.72
13	0.7	0	4.477	2.996	1.06	28	0.7	0	5.328	3.912	1.25
14	25.9	0	5.236	4.942	1.30	29	13.4	0	5.802	6.685	1.08
15	54.9	1	6.151	6.752	1.52	30	5.5	0	6.176	4.787	1.25

**Example 15.2
(cont.)**

Logistic regression can be used to model the relationship between the response variable, log odds of the proportion of acceptable cheese, and the three explanatory variables, ACETIC, H2S, and LACTIC. Specifically, the model is

$$\log(odds) = \beta_0 + \beta_1 ACETIC + \beta_2 H2S + \beta_3 LACTIC.$$

To perform this logistic regression, follow these steps.

1. Click **Statistics**, click **Regression**, and then click **Logistic**. The SPSS window in Figure 15.2 appears.
2. Click *tasteok*, then click ▸ to move *tasteok* into the "Dependent" box.
3. Click *acetic*, *h2s*, and *lactic*, then click ▸ to move *acetic*, *h2s*, and *lactic* into the "Covariates" box.

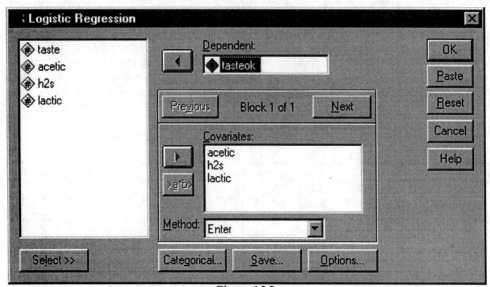

Figure 15.2

4. If you are interested in a confidence interval for the odds ratio, click the **Options** box. Click the **CI for exp(B)** option, and then click **Continue.**
5. Click **OK**.

Table 15.5 is part of the resulting SPSS output.

```
Dependent Variable..    TASTEOK

Variable(s) Entered on Step Number
1..         ACETIC
            H2S
            LACTIC

                      Chi-Square      df Significance

    Model                 16.334       3      .0010
    Block                 16.334       3      .0010


-------------------- Variables in the Equation ----------------------

Variable           B       S.E.      Wald    df      Sig        R      Exp(B)

ACETIC           .5844    1.5442     .1432    1     .7051    .0000    1.7940
H2S              .6848     .4040    2.8729    1     .0901    .1584    1.9834
LACTIC          3.4684    2.6496    1.7135    1     .1905    .0000   32.0845
Constant      -14.2599    8.2867    2.9612    1     .0853
```

Table 15.5

Example 15.2 (cont.)

From the output the fitted model is

$$\log(odds) = -14.26 + 0.58\,ACETIC + 0.68\,H2S + 3.47\,LACTIC.$$

Initially, we examine the null and alternative hypotheses H_0: $\beta_1 = \beta_2 = \beta_3 = 0$ and H_a: some β_i differs from 0. This hypothesis is tested using the Chi-square statistic for the model. Since the test statistic $\chi^2 = 16.33$ (df = 3) and the P-value < 0.0001, we reject H_0 and conclude that at least one of the explanatory variables can be used to predict the odds that cheese is acceptable. Further analyses are necessary to determine the explanatory variable(s) that results in the best model. These analyses are assigned in IPS homework exercises 15.9, 15.10, and 15.11.